Dispat

An Americ.... Family Spends 3 Years

Living in England

By Nicole Wiltrout

Acknowledgements

To our family (Guy, Diane, Tom, Zoe, Renee, Adam, Jake, Tara, Andrew, Emily, Frances, and Cousin #4) and our friends: Knowing we always had you to welcome us home was a constant comfort to us. Your love and support made the Atlantic feel smaller than it was.

To the friends we made in England: So many of our conversations fueled various topics for this book. We saw wonderful places while living abroad, but by far our best experience was meeting you. xx

A special thanks to Jonathan Thomas, for letting me post on Anglotopia each week, forgiving my typos, and then providing an opportunity for this book to be published.

This book is dedicated to my sons, Ben and Jonathan. Without you by my side, every trip and story that came from it would have felt empty. You won't remember much of the three years we lived in England, but it changed you in immeasurable ways.

And to my husband, Jeff. Thanks for encouraging me to pursue every dream I've ever had. No adventure would have seemed possible without your courage, and no experience would have seemed worthwhile without you to share it with. I hope I'm holding your hand on park benches around the world for many more years. Who's got it better than us?

Introduction

If you're opening this book, we already share something in common: a love for England, both the country and its people. This book is a chronicle of many things (from how I navigated English grocery stores to how I learned to drive), but I hope the most important feeling it conveys is how I fell in love with this place.

Unlike some of you, I would never have considered myself an Anglophile before I moved to England. I never watched *Downton Abbey* (gasp!) or had a proper afternoon tea (the horror!). I had only been to London once, for three days while in college as part of a larger whirlwind tour through Europe, as you do when you're 21: full of energy and a desire to see the world.

Throughout the coming decade, my need to travel and explore new places never wavered, and even when my husband and I welcomed two children into the world we continued to travel and dream of a chance to move internationally at some point in our lives.

In late 2012, with a fussy baby on my lap and my toddler crashing matchbox cars by my feet, my husband sent me a text that read along the lines of, "I was just offered a chance to move here. What do you think?" He was on a business trip in England. And our lives changed forever.

Throughout the next 5 months, as we spent hours upon hours planning and then executing an international move with two young children, my emotions ranged from pure terror to uncontrollable excitement. (I was rarely in a calm place in between those two feelings.) This range of emotion continued throughout our first year living there. In hindsight, it was perfectly natural. I've read many articles about the stress that expatriates face, particularly those with children.

As you read this book, which is a compilation of posts I wrote each and every week of our time living in England from beginning to end, you'll likely notice the full range of all of this. At certain moments, I was frustrated: there was so much to learn, everything was different, and it seemed like something went wrong each and every day. I swallowed a lump of homesickness stuck in my throat more times than I can count. But at other moments I could see so clearly how wonderful this opportunity was, and how fortunate we were to be given this chance.

This book isn't a how-to tutorial about moving to the UK. We had a special situation whereby my husband's company took care of the immigration process for us. I honestly don't know the details of that, other than having to spend about 20 minutes in an immigration office a couple of months before we moved to get our visas. Entertaining small children on transatlantic flights? That I consider myself an expert on!

But what I do hope it gives you is a glimpse into the experience of an American family, picked up from their Indiana home and dropped off in a small English village, and their transformation from complete naiveté to relative confidence with the English way of life. We learned so much and had many a laugh about all the mistakes we made.
In 2001, as a 21-year-old traveler through Europe, I thought England was nothing more than flashy red double decker buses and the famous sites of London buzzing by my face. By February of 2016, when I saw the church steeples of my town in the rearview mirror of our car for the last time, tears streaming down my cheeks having just hugged my dear friend goodbye, I knew it was so much more than that. It's a country that has captured my heart and my imagination, and I'll think of it fondly each and every day. I hope by writing this that I'll have shared a piece of that personal journey with all of you as well.

Life in the UK

Three Things I Love About My British House

Over the course of two housing visits to England during our relocation process, my husband or I walked through at least a dozen or so properties. We quickly learned that there are some major differences between American and British homes (beyond average square footage, which won't surprise anyone who has watched House Hunters International). But I've learned to love a lot about my home here. (I'll share what I loathe in my next article!)

Our Conservatory

What's a conservatory, you ask? It's a popular way to add on to a home here. Basically, it's a porch area enclosed by glass walls and a glass ceiling, making it usable year-round (although it does get a bit warm during the hot days we've experienced this summer). For our family, we've made our conservatory a playroom for our two boys, ages 1 and 4. It means they get to play in an area with a lot of natural light flooding in, and the tile floor means I don't have to worry about spills and messy play. And while it does take away some space from our garden, given the unpredictable weather here, I have no doubt we'll make better use of this space throughout the year.

Our Garden

This is what Americans would call a yard. It's almost standard that gardens here are completely enclosed. This was unlike my yard in the US.

Now my sons are free to play outside as often as they wish, without needing my constant supervision to ensure they don't run out into the street. Our garden here has high walls on each side, which provides a lot of privacy. While I do miss the friendly banter I'd have with neighbors in the US on nice weekends when we'd all be out grilling, it's nice to know my family has some space that is completely our own.

My Dishwasher

What a silly thing to love, right? But I had grown so frustrated with my US dishwasher, which often spit out dishes that hardly looked clean and were covered in a white dust.

Here, my dishes come out absolutely spotless and shiny, even when I don't rinse as well as I should. I have no idea what the difference is, perhaps the detergent that's used? Whatever it is, I love it.

Three Things I Hate About My British House

My last post detailed some of what I love about my home here in England. And truly, I do love our house here. In fact, if I had to choose between my home in the US and my home here, I'd pick this house in a heartbeat. But... that doesn't mean there aren't a few sacrifices we've made in terms of housing amenities when we moved across the pond. I've outlined my pet peeves below.

The Washer and Dryer

If I could change anything about my house here, I'd change these two appliances. With four members of our family, including two messy little boys, laundry is a constant in our lives. My British washer and dryer can only fit about half of what a load in the US would consist of. And it probably takes about twice as long to run the washer, and the dryer can be even more time-consuming. It's no wonder that on nice days, you'll see laundry hanging to dry at even the poshest homes around here. I've gone from doing about 3-4 loads per week in the US to 6-7 loads per week here. And that's even after I've considerably changed my standards as to what is truly "dirty."

The Windows

Now, in general, there's nothing wrong with our windows. They open easily, let in cool breezes on warm days, and provide a beautiful view of the English countryside. But do you know what they lack? Screens.

Meaning in the nice months, when I want to savor the beautiful air, I have a huge bug problem. I'm constantly killing little creatures of all shapes and sizes. Yuck! While I'm thankful that there are no mosquitos here, I'd prefer to not feel like I'm camping all summer. And so I end up keeping my windows closed more often than I'd like to.

The Garage

We knew we'd have to say goodbye to our spacious two-car American garage. But I know this winter I'll miss getting into my relatively warm car that was protected from the elements all night. In fact, most Brits use their garages for storage or as a workshop. Rarely do you see cars actually parked in them. And while I don't know if this is typical, our garage is attached to our house but we have no access to it from within our home. Seems so unusual to me!

But like I said, in general, we love our home here. I know I will miss it when this experience comes to an end in a few years. I will, however, happily reunite with my American washer and dryer!

Life in an English Village

One of the common misnomers Americans make when you tell them you're moving to England is that they assume you'll be living in London. But just like the US is so much more than just New York and LA, there is life beyond London here.

In fact, the population of England is 53 million people. And just over 8 million people reside in London. Many of us find ourselves living in small villages. These can vary in population from 15,000 (the largest) to 40 or so (smallest). My village, Collyweston, has 400 people. So what defines village life? Naturally, they're each a bit different, but there are some typical commonalities.

A Village Shop

Sometimes called a corner shop. Again, they vary in size (often corresponding to the size of the village, naturally). They carry typical grocery items, like milk, bread and snacks. Some offer freshly prepared foods like sandwiches or ready-made meals. Sometimes there is a post office window (very handy for shipping letters and packages back to the US)! My kids love that our shop has a nice variety of sweets to choose from, and taking a walk to the shop for a treat is something we do at least once a week.

A Pub

This, along with the shop, is often the hub of socialization in a village. Many serve food, and often they have rooms you can rent for the evening. (In other words, a combination of bar, restaurant, and bed & breakfast.)

A Village Hall

Sometimes it's the village's church or some other type of public meeting space. Some village halls are more active than others. At the hall, you might find exercise classes, craft clubs or other group meetings.

Other things you'll find in my village? A small cemetery. A playground and playing fields. A church. We even have our own monthly newsletter, so you're always up to speed on what's going on.

Villages often spring up as you're driving through the countryside. One moment you're cruising along at 60 mph and then suddenly you see signs cautioning you to slow to 30 or 40 mph. The landscape abruptly changes from wheat fields or sheep pastures to homes stacked neatly against each other for a kilometer or two. And just as soon as you come upon it, you're through it and back to cruising speed again.

I feared village life would seem isolating and lonely. Despite being a Midwestern girl, I've never lived out in the country before, always in towns of at least 20,000 people or so. Instead, I find it to be very social. Neighbors are interested in meeting their neighbors. The people who work in the shop are always quick with a greeting and the sharing of local news. The bartender in our pub knew us after just a couple of visits.

And within just a few weeks, our little English village sure felt like home. If you're planning a trip to the UK, be sure to incorporate some time in your itinerary to explore a few villages. It'll give you a sense of what life is like for Brits living outside the city limits.

The Kindness of Strangers: Are The English Welcoming?

Before moving to England, I had braced myself for a change in personal interactions. The Brits are a tough nut to crack, one person told me. They're not as friendly as folks in the Midwest are, someone else said. You'll be lucky to meet your neighbors, another added. (These were all people who were either British themselves or who had spent a lot of time in the UK, so they had some authority, I figured.)

But I have found the total opposite to be true. My family has been treated so well here. A few examples:

Within the first two days of moving into our house here, every single neighbor on our street came over to say hello and introduce themselves. There were offers to babysit our kids, many "please come knock on our door if you need anything" comments, and suggestions for fun outings or places to visit. Our relationship with all of them has continued to progress and I suspect we'll be good friends by the time we leave.

During one of my initial trips to the grocery store, when I was still using my US credit card, the machine wouldn't accept it at the checkout. With two whining and confused kids and a full cart, the manager of the store made me hand over my bags and instructed me to find an ATM. (Ok, so admittedly, he wasn't a good example of kindness!) I walked away in tears, ready to just give up and go home without any food.

But the woman who had been behind me in line found me at the entrance to the store and helped me find an ATM down the block.

One afternoon I took my kids to our village's playground. I began chatting with a grandmother who was there with her granddaughter and she invited me to a playgroup that meets in the next village. I wasn't able to go, but two weeks later, as I was walking down the street with my kids, I noticed a car suddenly stop and pull to the side. That same woman got out and walked toward us to let me know that the playgroup was planning some summer outings. We exchanged contact information and then she walked back to her car and was on her way. I can't imagine anyone in the US stopping their car to make sure I was in the loop on upcoming social events!

All of this is in addition to friendly and frequent chats in the store with staff and fellow shoppers, an almost weekly greeting by my postman, and so many more examples of friendliness and warmth. Don't let anyone tell you differently: the English are very welcoming. I only hope I'll have many chances to pay it forward in the years to come.

Grocery Shopping, a US vs GB Throwdown

One of the biggest challenges for me in adjusting to life in England is grocery shopping. It seems simple, right? You show up at the store, find what you want to eat, then pay for it and head home. But if you've ever been an expat in a foreign country, then you'll know it's not nearly as straightforward as that. So this month, the Dispatches from England column will focus on grocery shopping in Great Britain.

First up is a breakdown of who does it better. This will give you a sense of how different the experience is and perhaps a better appreciation of the transition I've made. Next week, I'll cover the similarities. I'll also write about the various stores there are to choose from, as well as some surprising finds and observations (at least to this American shopper).

United States vs. Great Britain Grocery Shopping Throwdown

Shopping Carts: Advantage US

If I could change one thing about living in Great Britain, I would change the shopping carts at the grocery store. I know this sounds extreme and completely ridiculous, but they are absolutely impossible to steer. All four wheels are on a swivel and I have so much trouble controlling them. It only gets harder as you add weight (like the 30-pound toddler who is always sitting in the front basket, not to mention all the food a family of four eats).

At first I thought I must be doing something wrong, but as I looked around, I quickly observed the locals struggle just as much as I do. I often end my shopping trip cursing under my breath and missing my American grocery cart. David Cameron, if you're reading, I'd be happy to lead a committee about getting this situation rectified immediately! ;)

Ready-Made Meals: Advantage GB

The pre-made food in the US is often nothing more than a pile of roasted chickens that have been sitting under a heat lamp for hours, or a pile of frozen pizzas crusted with ice. (I love you, America, but seriously.) Not here. You can find anything from amazing Thai curries to gourmet beef Wellingtons. I enjoy cooking, but I hate having to do it 7 nights a week. I rely on these types of pre-made meals at least a couple of times each week. I'm convinced the US would be healthier if we had these options, which are just as easy as a trip through the drive-thru.

Online shopping and delivery: Advantage GB

The prevalence (and relatively low-cost) online ordering and delivery is amazing here. Nearly all the major stores offer it, and often, if you pay attention to deals and special offers, you can score the delivery for free. You simply hop online, order your groceries, and choose a delivery time. And then, voila! A driver shows up at your door during your chosen time slot with all your food. It is absolutely brilliant and I will miss it tremendously when we move back. I'm hoping the US will get on board with this trend before that happens. (I know it exists in some big cities in the States, but I never lived anywhere that offered it, at least not for a reasonable price.)

Frequency of shopping: Advantage US

For reasons I still can't quite process, I find myself
shopping much more frequently here. (Which I
dislike. Maybe some people enjoy grocery shopping?
If so, teach me your ways!) In the US I typically made
one big run each week, and only occasionally had to
duck into a store at one other point during the
week to get a few things. Here, I typically either go to
the store or order online twice per week, and
sometimes I still have to make a supplemental trip to
the village shop to fill in the gaps. One factor I think
is the size of much of the packages of food here.
They're just smaller, understandably, as most people
here have smaller refrigerators and cabinet space for
storing food.

Shopping Experience: Advantage GB

The grocery stores here are quite nice. Many have
cafes or coffee shops. The employees, for the most
part, are very professional and helpful. I find the
produce quality and freshness to be outstanding.
Aside from the grocery carts, going to the store is
typically a more pleasant experience. Once I find
what I'm looking for, anyway.

Range of Product Options: Advantage US

Picky about a particular brand of x, y, or z? Better get
over it. The number of options for each product is
much more limited here. So no, you won't find a
hundred cereal options. Thirty or so will have to do.
This hasn't bothered me, as I think it simplifies the
shopping experience, but I know that for some
Americans it might be frustrating.

How Grocery Shopping is Similar in the UK to Shopping in the US

As a follow-up to last week's post, a throwdown between US and GB grocery shopping experiences, I wanted to share how shopping for food is similar here. Seems we're not so terribly different after all.

Checkout

At most of the stores, you'll find both the self-checkout (perfect if you've just got a few things), and the more traditional conveyor belt with cashier. They also have the little plastic markers to differentiate your purchases from the person behind you in line.

Bags

Shoppers are encouraged to bring their own reusable bags, much like you find in the US. In fact, at some of the stores you receive a few pence off your bill or points on your loyalty program if you do. They also sell nicer bags for you to use should you neglect to bring any. And they'll typically ask if you want to bag your items yourself or not.

Coupons

You can find coupons in various places (although I've yet to find many in the Sunday paper, like you'd find in the US) Often, after I check out, some coupons will print out along with my receipt.

The stores themselves frequently offer deals like price matching, vouchers for free delivery, etc. Anyone know where I can find more coupons like I was used to clipping in the paper each week? I'm always looking to save a few quid.

Store Organization

The stores are set up quite similar to the US Produce is usually the first section you walk through, just to the right of the entrance. Cold and frozen items are in the back or off to the side, and the middle is full of the usual packaged goods, like soup cans, cereals and biscuits. The aisles are labeled with signs above describing what you'll find.

Other Services

Like some US stores, you may also find other smaller businesses inside, like watch repair, a small banking branch, or a cafe.

Loyalty Programs

Several of the stores offer loyalty programs to shoppers who frequent their stores. My favorite is Nectar, because I can use it at Sainsbury's (a large grocery chain), Homebase (a home goods chain), Expedia, and several other shopping outlets and websites. Basically, I earn points each time I shop at one of these places. I can then use the points on travel, money off my bills, etc. I know there are similar programs in the US.

Also, don't forget to bring a £1 coin with you. At most stores, you'll need one in order to access a cart (much like the US store Aldi).

UK Grocery Store Surprises for an American

Continuing on with my grocery store theme this month (I've already covered who does it better and similarities), this week I'm sharing some grocery store surprises. Or, things that might shock an American, anyway.

Eggs are not refrigerated. This is a difference I still shake my head at each time I pick up a container of room temperature eggs. Being the American I am, I quickly get them in the fridge as soon as I get home. I know it's completely fine, I just can't seem to get used to it. And you have no idea how long it took me to the find the eggs the first time I went shopping. I scoured every refrigerated area of the store until I was so frustrated I asked someone. Who knew they'd send me to the baked goods aisle?

Speaking of refrigeration, there's **a sign by the bananas in most of the stores encouraging people not to refrigerate their bananas**. Apparently some people must do that?

If you get anything from the butcher or the fishmonger, **they'll send you off to finish your shopping while they wrap up your order**. As I stood there waiting for my piece of halibut the first time I ordered some fish, the woman working there looked at me like I was crazy and quickly realized I had no idea what I was doing. Off she sent me to finish my shopping. Like most Brits, at least she was quite polite about it, although I'm sure she was chuckling at my ignorance.

You may get handed a small token at the end of your shop. Or slip of paper. These are charity programs. For instance, if you spend a certain amount at Waitrose, the cashier will hand you a small green token. As you leave the store there are several bins, each representing a different charity. When you drop your token in a particular bin, Waitrose will make a donation to that charity. Don't confuse the token as being a perk or loyalty thing and try to use it as a discount coin the next time you shop. Only silly Americans would do something like that. *cough*

The cashier will not begin scanning your items until you completely unload your cart. I'm still not quite sure why this is, but the first few times I shopped, it was incredibly awkward. I assumed I was doing something wrong until I got the hang of it. And I still fumble around a bit when there's not enough space on the conveyor belt for all my purchases to fit. I usually just ask them to start scanning anyway.

Don't let your kids stand on the end of the cart. Excuse me—*trolley*. I usually let me 4-year-old stand on the step at the end of the cart as we move around the store in the US. (He was always careful and I kept a close eye on him.) I was quickly scolded at a store for allowing him to do that. *Tsk, tsk*. So no more of that!

A Guide to Major British Grocery Store Chains

I hope you're enjoying reading about my experience learning the ins and outs of grocery shopping in Great Britain. In particular, my post comparing the US and GB drew a lot of attention. Clearly everyone has a strong opinion on where to shop here. So I thought I'd finish the month-long theme of groceries with a brief description of some of the major chains.

I should preface this by saying that these are merely my opinions. You may prefer one store over another for very different reasons. Also, these are the stores I have personal experience with. There are several other major chains found in Great Britain, but not anywhere near where I live, and thus I haven't shopped at them yet. In alphabetical order to be fair:

ASDA: This is the UK equivalent to Walmart (owned by Walmart, in fact). You'll find it a bit smaller than a US Walmart store, but otherwise fairly similar. I'd estimate that about 2/3 of the store is made up of food, and the other 1/3 is non-food products, like clothes, books, toys, home goods, etc. I only go occasionally, mostly because it carries the British version of Goldfish crackers (called Finz here) that my children really miss from home.

Marks and Spencer: This is both a grocery chain and a department store (the grocery version being called M&S Simply Food). There is one near my house and I love visiting, mostly for their quality ready-made meals.

In fact, they run a popular deal called 2 for £10. You get a main entrée, a side dish, a dessert and a bottle of wine, all meant to feed two people, for £10 (approximately $15). Can't beat that price, and the quality is great.

Morrisons: I shop here somewhat regularly. The prices are pretty consistently low, and as it is one of the larger stores near my house, the selection is really great. I also enjoy that it has a salad bar (somewhat unusual here but something I love for lunch) and a large cafe.

Sainsbury's: This is where I tend to do the bulk of my shopping. It is somewhat similar in size to Morrisons, but has the added benefit of online ordering and delivery. Plus, this store participates in the popular Nectar loyalty program. Since food is a big expense for my family, I like earning points when I shop. Plus, it is conveniently located next to my son's nursery school, so I drive by it often.

Tesco: This is a very popular chain of stores here, but I don't have one close to where I live so I've only shopped there once. There is a miniature version nearby, called Tesco Express, that I pop into occasionally, but it's not large enough for me to do my weekly shopping run there.

Waitrose: This is another very popular choice here. It is a bit smaller than some of the other stores, but the quality is fantastic, especially the ready-made meals, meat and produce. They also offer online ordering and delivery. I find their prices a bit high, but if I'm making a special meal then I make it a point to come here for most of the ingredients.

Again, this is not intended to be a comprehensive listing of British grocery stores. I'm well aware that I've missed a few big ones. Nor would I ever try to convince anyone to shop where I shop. It's simply my experience learning and discovering what feels most comfortable to me.

My First British Parking Ticket

I got my first parking ticket here this week. It made me so angry that I figured I better make some good come from it. So I turned it into a blog post topic for my Dispatches from England column this week.

Most Americans probably think that the biggest adjustment you make when learning to drive across the pond is adjusting to driving on the opposite side. I certainly thought so. And yes, that's a big change. So are the roundabouts, the narrow roads, the different road signs, etc. I'll be writing a lot more about our process of learning to drive, particularly as my husband and I start the process of obtaining our UK driver's licenses.

But here's a change I didn't anticipate: parking difficulties. Let's talk about some of the differences.

First, **it's called a car park here**, not a parking lot. That's the easy part.

The spaces, much like the streets, are very narrow. Yes, the cars here are typically smaller than our super-size American cars. And while we drive two European-sized cars, I still find that I typically can't open my car door all the way for fear of hitting the car next to me.

On the plus side, many retail stores that have their own dedicated car parks **offer wider spaces for those driving with small children** in the back seat. If you've ever had to get a baby or toddler in and out of a car seat, then you'll understand why a few extra inches which allow you to open your car door all the way is enormously helpful.

Not to mention they're typically closer to the store entrance, making carrying kids to and from the car much easier as well. I wish more stores in the US offered this, quite frankly.

Don't plan to get around a car park quickly. Many people here **prefer to back into the parking spaces** and I often find myself patiently waiting for them to do that so I can move ahead. I assume this is to make it easier when the time comes to leave. I've never been that great at backing into a parking space (particularly a small one), so I still usually just pull in. (I do have some pretty amazing parallel parking skills, which I've used often here.)

You'll typically have to pay. The town or city-owned car parks around where I live are usually what's called "pay and display." Meaning once you've parked your car, you walk over to a machine, pay a few pounds, and it prints you a ticket. You then leave that ticket on your windshield. In Stamford near where I live, £1.80 (equivalent to roughly $3) will get you 3 hours of time at most of the car parks. We have to pay to park at nearly all our local parks and playgrounds, too. So a free trip to the playground is a thing of the past (for us, at least).

You can park along the side of just about any street. I'm often amazed that I'll be driving along on a road where the speed limit is 60 mph and suddenly there's a car pulled over slightly completely stopped. It's simply parked in front of a house or a footpath or a shop. I would never dream of parking on a major road with a high speed limit in the US, but here it is common practice. I also often see cars parked along busy roads in Stamford, too, and traffic slows to a crawl as cars can only get through one at a time.

Since I'll still a little unsure of the rules, I tend to seek out the car parks instead of parking street-side.

So why did I get my first ticket? Allow me to release a bit of frustration over this. I was parking in a town car park. I had my toddler in the back seat, along with a friend and her baby. Since I wanted us to be able to open both back doors fully to make it easier to get the two young kids out of the back, I intentionally drove to the furthest away point of the car park, where there were relatively few cars parked. I paid my fee, then walked back to the car to start getting the kids out. I noticed that my front left tire was slightly over the line and into the space next to me, but I didn't think it was a big deal since there were no other cars nearby. And someone could easily have still parked in the space next to me. Alas, I returned a couple of hours later to find a £50ticket (roughly $75). Fortunately, if I paid it immediately, it was reduced to £25. I wasn't happy about it (after all, there was in fact a car parked in the spot that I was supposedly intruding on), but I paid it. And I'll definitely be sure to keep my car in the lines from here on out.

British Things I'll Miss When I Move Back to America

In some ways it is hard to believe it's been over six months since my family moved to England. We've adjusted fairly well. My sons are both settled into school and nursery. Our house is really comfortable for us, and driving no longer makes me a nervous wreck. We've gotten to know a few people, and overall, it feels more like home than it did our first few weeks.

I know that our three years here will go by quickly. I've already been thinking about what I'll miss from the experience that can't be replicated back in the US. Here are a few:

Our Village

I wasn't sure how I'd feel about living in a small village. I thought it would be isolating. But we really do love it here. There's really nothing to compare it to in the US. Living out in the country in America often means you're miles away from a store, or a restaurant, or even any neighbors. For some, this remoteness is probably exactly what they desire,but I know I'd feel lonely. Here, I can walk to our shop, the pub, and a park. If I look out the window on one side of my house, I can see nothing but rolling fields for miles. Out the other window, I can practically shake hands with my neighbor. It's such a lovely combination of peace and tranquility, but without losing a sense of community.

The Food

Sure, there is a lot of food from the US that I crave. But for each American product I miss, there's easily a British food that I've fallen in love with. I plan to devote an entire post to this soon, but let's just say I've had to scale back some of my indulgences after putting on a few pounds when we moved here.

They're Not Workaholics

Perhaps this is true all over Europe, and not just in Great Britain. But I find people here take their time away from work seriously. They plan fun holidays. They attend festivals. They have hobbies, like cycling or hiking or knitting. I know this is true in the US too, but I often felt like I heard Americans boasting about not taking all of their vacation time and working all weekend. As if that was better than putting the laptop away for a couple of days and spending quality time with family or friends. People here value their personal time more, and I really like that about the culture.

Politeness

Overall, people here are quite polite. Even if you barely brush shoulders with someone on the street, they'll apologize. Cashiers at the store probably thank me at least 3 or 4 times when I make a purchase. When I first moved here, I had a very frustrating experience getting our phone and internet set up at our house. Each day for several weeks, I was on the phone with a representative from the company (which I shall not name for fear they'll cut me off from the outside world). I wanted desperately to yell at them and complain.

Yet they were so polite even while delivering bad news that I felt I couldn't be mean about my unhappiness. I like the sense of being respectful that exists here instead of the sometimes harsher approach in the US.

Public Transit

I should preface this by saying it's probably not as prolific as you might think. Many Americans think you don't need a car to live anywhere in Europe. That's certainly true in some places in Great Britain, but I definitely need a car to live in my village, which only offers a weekly bus ride to the nearby town one day a week. But, to travel to London is only a 45-minute train ride away for me. And if you book ahead, it's usually only $15-25. Considering you'd easily spend that much on gas, not to mention the cost of parking in London, that's a real bargain and a time saver (the city is at least 2 hours away by car). Plus, I love getting to enjoy the city without having to drive through it! I can easily get to a nearby major airport and several other cities via the train as well. I'll miss that ease of travel.

Just a few things that will make the transition back to the US difficult. Luckily I still have 2 ½ more years to enjoy them!

A Few Things from America that I Miss While Living in the UK

Last week I shared just a few of the many things I'll miss about living in the UK when we move back to America. But as Dorothy said, "there's no place like home." So what do I miss about the US?

Family and Friends

Pretty obvious, but it's definitely the most difficult part of moving so far away from home. Luckily, there are many ways to keep in touch, like Facetime, texting, email, and more. But nothing beats a hug from your mom, lunch out with your sister, or watching your kids play with their cousins. This is the first time I've lived more than an hour from my immediate family, and it's definitely been my biggest adjustment. Fortunately, we've already had a lot of visitors, with a few more scheduled in the months to come.

Good Mexican Food

There are a lot of American food products I miss, but at least some of it can be shipped over to us or brought back in a suitcase from time to time. But what I wouldn't give for a quality Mexican restaurant nearby. We used to eat Mexican out almost weekly when we lived in the States. We have made do by cooking it at home, or eating at the American-based chain Chipotle every time we go into London. But as far as food goes, it's what I miss the most.

Wide Streets

I feel like I've learned to drive over here pretty well and fairly quickly. I started driving the very first day we lived here, and just forced myself to learn. We're in the process of getting our UK driver's licenses now. But even though my comfort level with the roads here is growing, I still miss wide streets instead of the narrow, twisty roads I usually find myself on. Sure, they're charming. But it requires intense concentration and I always fear I'm going to take out my side mirror. And I'd love a few extra meters to work with when merging onto a large motorway.

Our Pediatrician

Let me be clear, I have no issues whatsoever with the NHS. I think it's very admirable that the UK provides universal healthcare to all its residents. The US could learn a lot from it. I also don't doubt the quality of the medical care here at all. But it is structured differently than what I'm accustomed to in the US. And so when my kids were really sick for two straight weeks, I found myself longing to see a pediatrician, a doctor who only treats children, instead of a general practitioner. But it was my only option. The doctor we were assigned didn't have a good bedside manner with young kids and didn't seem to enjoy treating them, either. (I also think that when your kids are sick, as a parent you're really vulnerable emotionally. I'm sure I missed the familiarity of home at that moment for many reasons beyond the doctor we saw.)

So that's the perspective of just one American who sometimes misses home. Just for fun, I thought I'd widen the circle and ask my husband and son what they miss, too.

Basketball

My husband played in a weekly basketball league. He really misses playing the game that he grew up with and the exercise. My sons and I miss going to watch him. We've been surprised by how easy it is to keep up with sports we love from the US (Although, often the games are on in the middle of the night!). But he misses opportunities to play himself. He'll just have to learn rugby or cricket!

String Cheese

This was from my 4-year-old, after he rattled off every member of our family, a handful of friends, and his preschool teacher. Once I told him I was curious what he missed besides people, this was all he could come up with. Such a shame, as the cheese here is so good. But he finds it too strong. His 2-year-old brother, on the other hand, can't get enough of it!

My Great British Pet Peeves (Or Pet Hates as the British Say)

I heard on the radio this week that January is the unhappiest month. I assume that's true just about everywhere. The fun of the holiday celebrations is over, the bills from all those gifts are rolling in, the weather is typically not very nice and spring is still quite some time away. In that spirit, I thought I'd channel my inner curmudgeon and share a few of the things that really annoy me since moving here.

Before I get a flood of comments from defenders of the British way of life, please know that I love it here. I adore so much about this experience, this culture, the people, everything. I almost feel guilty complaining about a few things. But naturally, anytime you undergo such a big life change, there are things that drive you a little nuts. And the most important reason I write this column each week is to share some of what I've observed that others might not have a chance to themselves.

Complaining About the Weather

I get it. Talking about the weather is part of the culture. And I know it rains a lot. But based on the comments you'll hear from many people here, you'd be convinced Great Britain has the world's worst weather, and I just don't agree with that. I first noticed it this summer when there were complaints about the heat.

The weather forecaster on television would say, "It's going to be another uncomfortable night." Mind you, it was barely hitting 70 degrees Fahrenheit. I know people say the heat is more significant because air conditioning is uncommon, but I assure you that I was never once tempted to turn on the AC in my house if we had it. And now that it's winter, I stand outside each afternoon waiting to pick my son up from school, listening to comment after comment about how cold it is.

Real cold is being frozen in your house with wind chills far below zero, like they've experienced this winter where I'm from. I typically wear a rain jacket and maybe a scarf. I hardly ever need gloves and I've only worn my heavy winter jacket twice since moving here. The weather here can at times be a drag. But that's true just about anywhere other than some tropical beach location. I actually find the weather here far more tolerable than other places I've lived.

Cold Toilets

This will show what a hypocrite I can be based on what I just wrote about complaining about the weather. But many bathrooms here have no heat. Places like fancy restaurants, public restrooms at the mall, even my own house. I've started to get used to it, but I have to say my 2-year-old still hates undergoing a diaper change in the cold.

The Time it Takes to Get Things Done

Some of the most basic things just take longer to complete here, plain and simple. Everything from dry cleaning some trousers to scheduling a doctor's appointment.

When we needed our internet turned on, it was a 3-week wait. It took 2 1/2 weeks for our car dealership to get a new wheel put on my car. We've been waiting well over a month for a new filter for our furnace because the company will only communicate via mail. I just had to schedule a simple house inspection for our lease, and the soonest they could get us in was mid-February. I've gotten used to these delays, but they infuriated me our first few months here.

Late Opening Times

I'm sure this one drives me crazy mostly because I have young kids, but many attractions don't open until 11 a.m., and some not until the afternoon. Because my youngest son naps for a couple of hours each afternoon, we like to do touristy things in the morning. We've never had a problem doing that in the US, where the latest opening time is usually 10 a.m. In the winter, the sun begins to set by 3:30 here, meaning if you don't arrive somewhere until noon, daylight hours for your visit will be limited. In a land where caffeinated tea and coffee flows like water, I can't understand why we can't open the doors by 9 or 10.

Inaccessibility

This is particularly a jab at the London Underground. I find it incredibly difficult to get around the Tube stations with a stroller. But beyond what's just an inconvenience to me, I'm sad to think about what those with a physical handicap must face in trying to navigate the city.

According to Transport of London, only 66 out of 270 stations on the Underground are step-free. I know it can be hard to modernize some stations given their age and historical significance. But many other European cities have found a way to do so, and I hope London will make it a bigger priority in the years to come.

Ok, complaining over. (And really, if the worst I can say about a place is that their loos are a little chilly, things could be much, much worse, right?) Back to enjoying this beautiful country and its way of life. I promise a more uplifting post next week!

Things My American Friends Ask Me About Life Here

I feel really lucky to be living as an expat in 2014. I'd imagine that it looks drastically different than it did even 10 years ago, due to the multiple ways I can stay in touch with friends and family back home. Hardly an hour goes by that I don't get a text, Facebook message, phone call or some other connection with people back in the US. It has made our move to England far less lonely for me.

Because it's so easy to communicate, I get lots of questions from friends back home about life here. I've been keeping track of some of these and thought I'd share a few.

What was the media coverage like of Prince George's birth?

I was pretty stunned when I first saw the hundreds of reporters camped out in front of the hospital before the Duchess of Cambridge even went into labor. I hadn't been hearing too much about her pregnancy in the major UK news outlets. And then it occurred to me that of course the US media was probably covering the story 24/7. My American friends just assumed that it was a huge story here too. And to be fair, it was,but not in the paparazzi kind of way.

It really wasn't in the mainstream news much until she actually went into labor, and the media seemed to respect the royal family's privacy much more than the US media probably did.

What's up with Nigella Lawson?

I was surprised to get this question, because I didn't think the celebrity chef was all that popular in the US. (I had watched one of her cooking shows on the Food Network a few times in the US, so I did know she was on television occasionally.) What I didn't realize is that she had begun starring on a primetime cooking competition in America since I left (called The Taste). If you haven't heard, two of her personal assistants were accused of fraud, and during the course of the trial she was accused of regularly using cocaine.

Is everyone talking about these NFL games being played in London?

Short answer: No. I happened to be in London the weekend one of the two games was played in the city, and yes, Regent Street was decked out in NFL flags and lots of people were walking around in various team jerseys. But we soon realized it was mostly American tourists. I knew a few people who went to the games; they were all fellow American expats. "American football," as it is called here, hasn't really taken off, at least among the folks I know. Although I'm proud to say that whenever it does come up in conversation, many Brits have heard of my beloved Indianapolis Colts.

Is the vaccination process the same?

The Los Angeles Times recently reported on the effects that the anti-vaccination movement has had on the spread of vaccine-preventable disease outbreaks, including a startling graphic that shows the prevalence of measles in Great Britain. This map quickly went viral on Facebook and my friends were wondering how vaccines work here.

Fortunately, my kids had received almost all of their vaccines in the US so I haven't had to personally deal with this much. But we were not able to get any member of our family a flu vaccine at our doctor's office because none of us fell into the high-risk categories. And the one vaccine that my youngest still needs is another hepatitis A booster, but that is also not typically available. The chicken pox vaccine is not commonly administered here either. (We could pursue private options for these.) But the other childhood vaccines, from my understanding, are readily available and follow a similar schedule.

Can you send a postcard to my child's school?

I LOVE this one! There must be a lot of teachers in America doing geography projects that involve collecting postcards or other mail from various places around the world. And I really enjoy contributing to it, as I like to picture the kids getting excited about finding England on the map.

A Guide to British Rubbish Collection

Often when I think about the cultural differences between the US and the UK (especially when I'm coming up with topics for this column!), I reflect in a "highbrow" way. How do people act, speak, treat each other? Music, television, culinary, and artistic differences?

But the reality is that the differences in lifestyle sometimes come down to the most basic things. Would you like to know the first thing I asked our neighbors after meeting them and exchanging pleasantries? "How does the trash collection work?" Yes. As basic as that. We had a nice laugh about how little I knew about living here (and that I didn't even call it by its proper name: rubbish bin).

So how does the trash collection work? I'll outline the similarities and differences below. (I should note that trash collection works differently around the US, and I'm sure it differs widely around the UK, too. I'm comparing my personal American experience with my personal British experience.)

DIFFERENCES:

- **Recycling and general trash alternate collection every other week.** So one week the recycling is picked up, the next week it is regular trash. The schedule is printed in my village's monthly newsletter and available online. A small bin for food scraps is collected weekly as well.

- **Size.** Our bin for general trash is half the size of the bin we had in the US (which was picked up weekly). So we have about 1/4 the size to work with, since it's only collected every other week. At first we were worried we wouldn't be able to fit everything, but we recycle so much that it hasn't been much of a problem.

- **Prevalence of recycling.** I'm embarrassed to say that my town in the US didn't offer recycling services. Instead, I had to drive my recycling to a collection site. Very inconvenient. Here, my recycling is picked up every other week, and I can combine everything into one big bin. No need to sort. Very easy.

SIMILARITIES:

- **A large trash truck** (that looks just like the one in the US that collected my trash) comes every Thursday morning to get either my trash or my recycling. It's usually a team or 2 or 3 men, one driving, and the others collecting the bins and dumping them in the back of the truck.

- **My trash in the US was collected by my town's public works department.** Similarly, my trash here is collected by my local council.

- **Heavy or large item disposal is available.** My town in the US had what we call a "dump," where for a small fee you could get rid of larger items that didn't fit or weren't appropriate for regular trash collection. Similarly, the nearby town here offers a

Saturday morning collection, where we bring any large items to be placed in big collection bins. This was especially nice for after the holidays, when we had some large boxes to dispose of.

And yes, my husband and I still argue about who should take out the garbage, regardless of which country we live in.

Tips for Preparing for a Dream Move to the UK

My family has only been living in England for just over a month now, but we spent nearly six months preparing for our move here. Here are a few tips that you can do in advance of a move to the UK, right from your very own home, to make life a little easier once you arrive.

Scan and make copies of all your important documents.

Passports, marriage certificates, birth certificates, even your US driver's license. You'll be asked for these often for all sorts of reasons both in the visa application process and establishing yourselves as residents once you've arrived. So make several paper copies and scan in an electronic copy so you'll always have them ready to go. Have children? Be sure to get their health records, including their immunizations.

Use co.uk web addresses.

If you're doing online research or shopping for UK products, use sites such as google.co.uk or amazon.co.uk. You'll get much better results in your searches than when using their dot com counterparts. And if you're using the Google Map feature, know that you can enter a postal code to view a specific location. Unlike in the US, a postal code here gets you within a few houses of any given address. This is helpful to know when house hunting online.

Plan ahead on email correspondence and be polite.

I have found, on average, that written communication here (both email and print) is much more formal and polite. So when I was emailing potential schools, our realtor, etc., I adopted a similar approach. First impression is everything, after all! Also, if you want a same-day or next-day response, be sure to email first thing in the morning. That will be midday here, so you stand a better chance of getting a quicker response.

Sign up for Groupon and/or Living Social deal sites.

Even if you don't plan to make any purchases through these sites (I didn't until after we arrived), you'll get a lot of ideas about things to do, places to eat, and even average prices for items around where you'll be living.

Network!

One of the advantages of moving to a country like the UK is that you may find that many friends, colleagues or acquaintances know someone who already lives here. I had many friends who sent me names and email addresses of people they knew, and I connected with each and every person suggested to me. You'll find they each offer a different area of expertise (schools, for instance, or driving lessons). And you'll have a much bigger pool of people to ask questions of as the move date draws nearer. I haven't used every single piece of advice offered up to me, but I'm very grateful for the connections I made in advance of our move.

3 Things You Need to Memorize When You Move to the UK

It's hard to believe it's already been a year since my family moved to England (we arrived June 1, 2013, or 1 June 2013 to my British readers!) So much about our first few weeks here was such a blur. Everything was new, we had so much to learn, and yet it was all so very exciting. And it still is exciting!

Upon arriving, I quickly realized there were a few numbers that I needed to memorize because I'd be asked for them all the time. If you're planning (or dreaming of) a similar move across the pond, here's what you should commit to memory first:

Your Postal Code

Unlike the US, where the same zip code is used for an entire town or a large portion of a city, in the UK your postal code practically pinpoints your specific home. Therefore, you'll be asked for it often. Giving someone directions to your house? All they need is a GPS (or Sat Nav) and your postal code, and it'll take them almost to your door.

I actually keep an entire note on my cell phone with a list of helpful postcodes (places we like to visit but don't travel to often enough to memorize exactly how to get there without our Sat Nav: friends' houses, restaurant recommendations, etc.) I also frequently use postal codes on Google Maps to determine the drive time when planning a road trip.

If you're planning some upcoming travel to the UK, it's helpful to know postcodes of all the places you want to visit, hotels, restaurants, etc. This probably seems very basic to UK residents, but to Americans who rarely use zip codes unless they're addressing an envelope, it's a foreign concept (No pun intended!).

Your License Plate Number

Called a number plate here, you'll sometimes be asked for this by a place of business when using their car park. Because car parking is much more limited (and therefore, often more tightly controlled), occasionally I'm asked for this information. I know some Americans know their license plate number by heart, but I never did. Even now, when I'm asked for it much more frequently, I still have to rack my brain to remember the letter and number combination.

Your Mobile (Cell Phone) Number and Home Number

This one is very obvious. But when I arrived, I was a bit overwhelmed to memorize two long and brand new numbers. In the US, I was so used to my area code that at least that portion of my phone number was always easy to remember.

Here, I suddenly had two 11-number sequences to learn. And when you first move anywhere, regardless of country, you fill out endless forms and paperwork. All of which ask for these numbers.

I was somewhat embarrassed those first few weeks to have to look down at my phone to pull up its number each time I was asked for it. Who doesn't know their own phone number, after all?

Details about the Actual Moving Process from the USA to the UK

I don't know why it has taken me over a year to document the details of how we actually moved our family and our belongings to the UK. Maybe I needed that much time just to recover from the stress of it! Anyone who has moved from one place to another knows that the actual process of moving is no fun. And the complications of making that move an international one is not for the faint of heart. *Note: this article is not about getting a visa, just the actual moving process.*

First, I'll explain how my family got here.

My husband came over to England for a few days about three weeks before our family was due to move here. He spent the bulk of that visit looking at rental properties. He selected his favorite, and my husband's company then worked on finalizing the lease. A week later, we sold our house in Indiana and moved into a hotel for a little over a week, and then lived with family for our last few days in the US.

On Tuesday, May 31, the day we were due to fly out, we got a phone call saying that the lease wasn't finished and that our house might not be available. We boarded our flight that afternoon anyway, without any idea as to where we would go once we landed.

That's a frightening situation, especially when you have two young children. (I will say, however, that my husband's company has been amazingly supportive to us throughout the process. I knew they wouldn't leave us stranded at Heathrow. But the unknown was still scary.)

When we landed, we were told to go to a temporary apartment in a nearby city and plan to be there for a few days. The lease still wasn't sorted out. Fortunately, a few days later, it was, and we eventually moved into the house we had originally planned to be in. It was such a relief, and 4 weeks after leaving our Indiana home, very nice to finally feel settled again. Compared to other expats I talk to, we actually had a pretty simple transition in terms of housing. Many expats live in temporary housing for much longer, or make several moves until they're settled in a permanent place.

So what about our belongings?

This was even more complicated, quite frankly. Basically, over a several week period, my husband and I slowly divided up our belongings into 5 different categories. They were: throw away/giveaway, storage, sea shipment, air shipment, or suitcases. The first is obvious. Since we were moving into a smaller house, we got rid of anything we felt we wouldn't need or didn't want to keep any longer.

My husband's company allowed us to store anything we didn't want to take to England. For us, this included a small piano and several pieces of furniture we knew we wouldn't have space for, things we hope to use again when we move back.

The sea shipment category is the main category that the bulk of our belongings went into. On the day the movers came to our Indiana home, they boxed up anything labeled "sea" and put it on a large semi-truck. That container was later transferred to a boat, which was then transported to England via cargo ship. Once it cleared customs, it was brought to our house here. In all, it took about six weeks to get most of our stuff. I'm told this is a really fast timeline.

The air shipment arrived much sooner. We had a weight limit on this, naturally, as it's incredibly expensive to ship via air. We used our allotted weight on some basic kitchen supplies so that I could cook, toys for our kids, and some additional clothes and shoes. It took about three weeks to get our air shipment (although because we had that shipped two weeks before we actually moved, we only had to wait about a week in England for it).

Otherwise, for that transition period, we lived out of five suitcases. Each family member had a small suitcase full of clothes and toiletries, and we had an extra suitcase full of toys and activities for our kids. Thankfully, my husband's company rented two small loveseats and three beds so that we at least had a place to sit down and to sleep at night for the month-long wait for the rest of our furniture. If I learned nothing else from that time period, I learned how much you really don't need most of the things you own. But I'll never forget the way the walls of our new house echoed for those first few weeks because it was primarily empty.

So that's how our move to England transpired. It was a complicated, stressful time, but so worth it in the end. The lasting image I have in my head is everything in our Indiana home, down to the books on our bookshelves and clothes in our closets, with a yellow post-it note that read "air" "sea" or "storage." I still laugh about that. Now I dread doing it all over again, in reverse!

Is Food Cheaper in the UK or the US?

Let's talk dollars and cents, shall we? One of the questions I'm most often asked is whether or not the cost of living is higher in the UK compared to the US. The very easy answer from my perspective is that it is definitely more expensive to live here in the UK. But I thought it would be interesting to take a look at how that plays out on a day-to-day basis.

So I did a little comparing of food prices. I created a list of commonly purchased items at the grocery store, and compared them head to head between the UK and the US. For fresh produce items, I also priced them out at my town's market day. One of the discoveries I made early on living here is that many products sold at the market were cheaper than the grocery store. (Unlike the US, where farmer's markets are sometimes more expensive than grocery store prices.)

To make these comparisons, I tried to find similarly sized items. While not always exact, I think these are close enough to make a fair comparison. I priced my groceries at the store I always shop at (while not the cheapest in the UK, it is known for relatively low prices). My sister priced these products at her local store in the US, with a similar reputation. I am listing the prices in US dollars, and used the Google pounds to dollar converter.

Milk (1/2 Gallon or 4 Pints):
UK Grocery Store: $1.60
US: $1.50

Eggs (1/2 dozen):
UK Grocery Store: $2.79
UK Market: $1.60
US: $1.08

Ground Beef/Beef Mince (1 pound):
UK Grocery Store: $7.20
US: $4.50

Apples (bag of 5):
UK Grocery Store: $1.60
UK Market: $1.60
US: $2.00

Bell Peppers (bag of 3):
UK Grocery Store: $2.39
UK Market: $1.60
US: $3.58

Multigrain Cheerios (small box):
UK Grocery Store: $3.99
US: $3.48

Coca-Cola (8 cans):
UK Grocery Store: $5.59
US: $3.88

I was actually surprised at some of these comparisons. While I find my food bill to be much higher here, I think that is largely due to the cost of processed foods and meat. Clearly, the produce is either similar in price or cheaper here in the UK. (It's also likely a big factor in why I cook with more fruits and vegetables now than I did in the US.) I plan to do this again in future posts, with things like household goods, electronics, etc.

A special thanks to my sister who helped me out with the research required on her side of the pond. And please, if you take issue with any of the prices listed, remember that food prices can vary greatly depending on where you live in the UK or in the US, and can also vary seasonally. So it may be that you can score a 1/2 gallon of milk for a buck where you live, but neither my sister nor I can. This was never intended to be a scientific study, just an overall look at food prices between the two countries.

British Things I Still Haven't Mastered Living in the UK

I recently had a conversation with some fellow American expats that made me realize just how much about life here in Great Britain that I still haven't figured out completely. When this group gets together, we often ask our embarrassing questions... cultural stuff we can't quite make sense of or need advice about how to handle. I've lived here for 18 months now, and here are a few things I still haven't mastered.

Tipping

Just when I think I finally have a handle on who to tip and how much, someone else gives me a different answer about that. For example, I recently had an awkward exchange with a new hair stylist when I tried to give her a £5 tip. (My haircut cost 40 pounds, so 5 seemed reasonable.) My previous stylist had always accepted the same amount, but this stylist refused it. So I polled the dozen or so expats at our meeting this week, and got about a dozen different answers as to how much or if they tip their hair stylist. I tend to get the same varying answers about this regarding how much to tip while dining out, whether or not to tip the takeaway delivery driver, how much to tip a taxi driver, etc. In fact, I can all but guarantee there will be comments on this post that will differ greatly about this topic.

(Just to be clear, I understand *why* there is a cultural difference between the US and the UK with regard to tipping. In the US, service staff sometimes make below the minimum wage and therefore rely greatly on tips. That's not the case here. Tipping is more centered on good service here, which makes sense. I just still can't quite figure out to whom and how much!)

Terminology

I've learned most of the differences in terminology at this point. I know my aubergines from my eggplants and my nappies from my diapers. But I often can't remember to use the British word! I had an interesting conversation with my 5-year-old son about this just the other day. As usual, I said pants and he said trousers. He then asked me, why, if we moved here at the same time, he uses English words but I still use American words. It made me realize just how much more quickly kids adapt to the language differences than adults do. I guess I'm just stuck in my old, American ways!

How to respond to "y'alright?"

(To slow it down... "you all right?") This is a common greeting in the area of England where I live. My first few weeks living here, I thought people were genuinely asking me how I was doing. But pretty soon I realized it was just their way of saying a quick hi or hello. Even though I know this, I still fumble with a response almost every time. Most people around here say, "Yeah, you?" but for some reason that just doesn't come out of my mouth naturally the way it does for the people around me. Instead I typically still say, "I'm fine, thanks," and then blush when I get strange looks.

Parking

At least I've managed to avoid getting any more parking tickets (knock on wood!), but I still have to double-check that I've managed to get my car completely in the lines in some of the narrower spaces. And I often have to try again, which can be a little embarrassing. I feel as though I rarely see British people checking to be sure they're in the lines; they just seem to know that they are. Maybe it's a skill I'll better acquire in my next year here.

Ending a Phone Conversation

Much like the "y'alright" greeting mentioned above, I tend to very awkwardly hang up on people when I make a phone call. In the US, once someone has said "bye" the call is over. Here, I often end up saying bye two or even three times before I feel comfortable hanging up without being rude. There's a hilarious Twitter feed called Very British Problems (@SoVeryBritish) that takes a funny look at some of these uniquely British quirks and it often mentions the awkwardness of ending a conversation here. So at least I'm not alone!

Surprising Things I Miss About the US

I've written before about some of the things I miss about the US. This list probably looks pretty similar to any American expat living in Europe's list. And frankly, very little of that surprised me. I sort of knew what I was getting into when we moved here. But when I was back in the US in August for a few weeks, and then upon returning to the UK, I realized a few things that I miss from "home" that really surprised me.

Corn on the Cob

To be honest, this one doesn't bother me a bit. I'm not a huge corn eater. But my children fell in love with eating corn on the cob when we were back in Indiana in August, and they begged me to make it when we got back. In the UK, corn is typically served frozen or out of a can (or on pizza and salads, actually). It's not as commonly sold on the cobs in the market or in the grocery store like you find in the US. My son was really disappointed that I couldn't find any of the cute corn on the cob holders that you can find in the US to make eating it easier. I remember asking a British friend who had moved to the US how her eating habits had changed, and she mentioned they eat a lot more corn now. I thought that was so strange, but now I understand! A buttery, salty cob just seems like a summertime rite of passage.

Crackers

Oh, how I miss Cheez-Its, Wheat Thins and Triscuits. Most Americans I know who live here say the same thing. And my children miss Pepperidge Farm Goldfish crackers. I used to be able to find Goldfish in some stores, although they were called Finz and tasted a little different, but now I can't find them. It's one of those foods that I just haven't found a suitable replacement for. The crackers here (called biscuits usually) are typically used for eating with cheese, so they're quite plain.

Resealable Packaging

This one is my husband's biggest pet peeves about living here. I never realized how efficient some US packaging is in terms of keeping food fresh. Deli meat and cheese, in particular, are very difficult to keep fresh once we've opened the package. In fact, the one thing I consistently ask visitors to bring us from the US is Glad Cling Wrap because I find I'm always using it to wrap up perishable goods once we've opened them. I miss the cling wrap from the USA because I don't find the UK version to be as good.

Sesame Street

You would think it would be my kids who miss this classic American show. But I think I miss it more than they do (it was my favorite, growing up). My youngest son was 16 months old when we moved here. I feel like he's the only American toddler who will never go through an Elmo phase. A new children's television show recently started showing here in the UK called The Furchester Hotel. It actually features a few characters from Sesame Street, like Elmo and Cookie Monster.

But it's just not the same and I find myself missing the fun, educational components and loveable characters from my childhood.

Colorful Fall Foliage

Autumn is very pretty here. In fact, I was just up in the Lake District a few weeks ago and it was positively gorgeous with the leaves changing color. But in the part of the US where I lived, fall colors are extremely vibrant. Bright reds, oranges, golden yellows, deep purples. The leaves do change color here, and it is pretty. It's just not as vibrant or as wide a variety of colors as you see in certain areas of the US.

The last time I wrote a post about what I missed from the US, someone commented that I should just move back there. So I'm bracing myself for some similar comments this time around. The truth is, we love living here. I write many Dispatches columns about all the things I enjoy about life in the UK. But I stand by the fact that there's absolutely nothing wrong with missing things from your home country, just as I'll miss many things about the UK when we move back.

Observations About British Weather

Weather. If there's one stereotype about British people that I've found holds very true, it's that they love to talk about the weather. When I first moved here, I was worried people didn't really like me or just weren't sure what to say to me, because the only casual conversations I had with strangers were about the weather. Now I understand that it's just part of the culture here.

So here are a few thoughts I have about the weather.

It's much nicer than I thought. I must admit, coming from Indiana, when the winter is absolutely frigid and the summer can be excruciatingly hot, I find the weather to be really pleasant here. You can spend time outdoors comfortably just about year-round, as long as you dress appropriately, yet you don't give up the seasonal changes that I really love.

That doesn't mean the weather is boring. In fact, it's quite unpredictable. A few of the strange things I've experienced for the first time here include fog that lasts all day, and straight into the next day. I've never before gone an entire day without the fog lifting even a little bit. So eerie. Because we live at the top of a hill, I've also experienced gale winds that last day after day. Particularly brutal in the winter, the wind is sometimes so loud at my house I have trouble listening to someone on the telephone.

And while I've had experiences of tornadoes coming within a mile or two of my house back in the US, this is my first time experiencing winds almost as strong that last beyond just an hour or two. On the plus side, I've seen more rainbows, including a double one, since moving here than my entire life combined. Beautiful!

While I regularly checked the weather forecast when I lived in the US, I rarely bother to do that here. I feel like it's hardly ever correct and since the weather changes minute to minute, we can usually delay outdoor plans by an hour or two if necessary. That's another thing I appreciate about British weather. Even when it rains, it rarely lasts all day.

A topic that often comes up with my fellow American expats is the cold here. If you were to compare the temperatures on an average winter day here versus where I'm from, it's typically colder in the US. But, on the other hand, the lifestyle here in the UK often requires that you be out in the elements for longer periods of time. In the US, if it was really cold out I would just dash into a store from the adjacent parking lot, or run my son into his preschool and run him back out when school dismissed. (If he had been older, I could have watched him wait for the bus from my living room window.) I could easily go throughout my day and only be outside for a few minutes, maybe even seconds, at a time.

Here, I typically park at least a 5-minute walk from most of the shops I need to get to. When I drop my son off at school, we stand around for 10 minutes waiting for the bell to ring, and a similar wait each afternoon to get him.

I'm usually outdoors for at least 30-40 minutes each day, if not more. I'm not complaining, I actually enjoy the fresh air. But it does make me appreciate spring's arrival just as much as I did in the US. Although at least here I don't have to worry about pipes freezing at my home if we're away, or frostbite setting in if I forget my gloves!

I enjoy summers back in Indiana, mostly for relaxing weekends around the pool and grilling out with friends and family. But I wouldn't consider it my favorite season there. However, here I find summers to be absolutely glorious. I think I've been lucky, in that the past two summers have been really nice and it's not always like that. But with temperatures at a very comfortable 70-80 degrees each day, and usually dry, I could spend the entire day outdoors with my family and hardly break a sweat. I will definitely miss summers here.

Thoughts on British Electrical Outlets

One of the first things you'll notice when arriving in the UK from America is that the electrical outlets look quite different. In fact, they don't just look different, they are different, operating on a different voltage altogether. I'm sure any tourist will have already read about this and prepared themselves by buying an adapter.

So what do I think of the British style of outlet? Here are a few thoughts

I prefer the three-prong style. I find this is sturdier, but at the same time easier to plug devices in and out. The American style always seems to require a bit of jostling about to get it to slide in properly. The two thin prongs appear flimsier to me.

I have a love/hate relationship with the on/off switch. On the plus side, I love that I can switch the power off to a certain plug. This was especially helpful since I moved here with very young and adventurous toddler. It added a level of safety I appreciated. (In addition to outlet covers, which I purchased after arriving here.) Plus, it seems less wasteful to not have electricity always at the ready at an outlet you don't ever use. But my knowledge of these things is admittedly quite limited. I'm sure a commenter can tell us if it actually does save electricity to shut it off!

But, on the other hand, I can't tell you how many times I've grabbed an electrical device assuming it was charged up, only to realize I had the switch off and it wasn't charged at all. There was also that time my 2-year-old shut off the switch to the outlet that was operating our hot water heater. We called a plumber out to see why we suddenly had no hot water. It never occurred to us to check that the outlet was still switched on. Oops.

I can understand that the UK and the USA would have a different system. But I do wish there was some uniformity between the UK and the rest of Europe. It makes traveling between the two complicated and requires packing more devices and cords than I'd like. About half of my electrical products are American, half British, meaning I bring several different adapters with me wherever I go, especially when traveling to continental Europe. Inevitably I forget one! (I recognize this is very much a first world problem, though.)

There are some devices that just won't operate properly even with an adapter. My son has asthma and uses a nebulizer from time to time. I'm always worried I might blow a fuse (or worse, burn up the machine) when I plug it in when we're traveling. Knock on wood, we haven't yet. When my sister-in-law met us in Paris over the holidays with her 5-month-old baby, she had to buy a new cord for her breast pump. And she would have needed another one had she come to our house in England! A hair dryer here will usually not work, even with an adapter. Fortunately, just charging up a phone or iPad is no problem whatsoever with an adapter.

You can get a converter, which is more expensive than an adapter but can handle the change in voltage more easily. (Or, for even more money, you can buy a transformer.) We heard so many horror stories from other expats who invested in these only to still have their expensive American electronics burn up that we haven't bothered, and instead bought new appliances here and left our American ones in storage. (Like toasters, televisions, vacuums, etc.)

Comparing UK and American Chain Restaurants

Many Americans think of the popularity of chain restaurants and stores (and the many independent places that struggle to compete) as a uniquely American problem. But it's actually an issue that both the US and Great Britain share (and I suspect many other countries around the world). I often read articles about the slow demise of the independent pub and the struggling high street shops and cafes here, much as I read articles about how Walmart is ruining America's independent stores.

We make an effort to eat at mostly independent places when we go out to eat here, but occasionally when traveling or when we just need a quick bite, we end up at a chain restaurant. So here are a few that we've patronized here in the UK, and how they compare to a US chain restaurant. *(I haven't listed every British chain restaurant, mostly because these are basically the only ones I've been to.)*

Nando's: The was the first chain restaurant that inspired this post, because the first time we ate there, my husband and I said to each other, "I think we've found the British BW-3's." Much like the popular American chicken wing restaurant, Nando's menu is centered around chicken, and you can pick your preferred sauce (to varying degree of spiciness) just like at BW-3s. Although the atmosphere in the restaurants is less sports bar and more of a casual family place. You will find several Nando's on the east coast of the US, also.

Pizza Express: Pizza Express is like an upscale Pizza Hut. The menu is mostly pizza, but also features pastas and nice salads, too. My kids really like this restaurant, in part because you can often watch the chefs work on your meal. I really enjoy eating here because the pizzas are quite good. The toppings are much nicer than a typical American pizza joint.

Pret A Manger: You'll find these all over the world, even in the US, although they're much more common here. I think their closest American counterpart would be Panera Bread. Relatively healthy food, served up pretty quick. We usually end up eating at these when we just want a quick snack or nibble, or sometimes we grab something to go before catching a train home from London.

Costa: I always say Costa is the UK Starbucks because you find them just about everywhere you go. (You'll find Starbucks here, too, although they're not nearly as prevalent as in the US.) Café Nero is another popular coffee shop chain here.

Frankie & Benny's: It would be easy to slip into a booth at Frankie & Benny's and convince yourself you were in Applebee's or TGI Friday's. It's a very American-style restaurant, and your kids will probably walk out with a balloon, too.

Bella Italia: Probably most similar to Olive Garden, although you won't find a bottomless salad or unlimited breadsticks on the menu. But Bella Italia caters very nicely to young children and so it's often a convenient option for my family.

After making this list, I think my greatest takeaway is how comparable the two country's chain restaurants are, and why it's so important to eat at independent places, too. Sometimes it's hard to avoid chains, especially with young children, but I know that Saturday lunches on the patio of my local pub will rank high on my list of memories from my time in the UK. Cups of coffee or meals at the places I've listed above probably won't.

Favorite British Wildflowers

I love the start of spring here in Great Britain. Actually, spring has always been my favorite season, but even more so now that I live here in England. For one reason, it seems to start a little earlier here than it does in Indiana, where I'm from (though summer will start a little later, so it all balances out). And I adore lambing season, which will start up in a few weeks. But primarily, it's because beautiful, colorful flowers begin to dot the fields and paths around my home. In fact, I can basically mark what month it is by seeing what's blooming around my village. A few of my favorite wildflowers where I live in the East Midlands:

Snowdrops

Do snowdrops exist in the US? I had certainly never heard of them. In fact, when my son came home from school last winter and told me he drew snowdrops for an art project, I had to Google it. But of course, now that I know what they are, I see them all around me this time of year. They are beautiful, darling little white flowers that dangle delicately from their stems, pointing down toward the ground, so they truly do look like a drop of snow. They begin to appear in late February and throughout March, so snowdrops come as a welcome sign that winter is retreating.

Daffodils

These have always been among my favorite flowers, in part because they're so cheerful, and also because in the US they typically bloom around my birthday in April.

I was quite familiar with them already, but they seem to be even more prevalent here in England. They also arrive about a month earlier. The stems are already shooting up around my village and I'm guessing it won't be long before their pretty yellow flowers are in full bloom. You can buy a whole handful of daffodils in any supermarket for only a pound this time of year, so they regularly fill vases in my windowsills. (The daffodil is also one of the symbols of Wales, and so you see people wearing the flower frequently around the St. David's Day holiday on March 1.)

Bluebells

I can't wait for the bluebells to start blossoming here (typically in April and May), as I recently discovered a parkland near my house that is supposed to be full of them when in season. We didn't know this place existed last year. I'm imagining a lot of family photos being taken when they do!

Buddleia

I spend hours and hours watching my kids play at our village's playground. Their favorite feature is the zip line, and there are huge bushes full of buddleia growing all around it. I will always associate this flower with the sounds of my children squealing with glee as they sail across the zip line.

Poppy

I know summer is in full swing when the red poppies appear. Now that I know the close connection between the poppy and the military, both British and American, in World War I, I will always count it among my favorites.

And because the field across the street from my house is full of poppies in the summer, which I can admire every time I look out my kitchen window, I will also always think fondly of the poppy and our time living here.

Maybe it's just part of the process of moving to a new place, but I love noticing what flowers are in bloom around me throughout the year here. I hope I'll bring that same level of awareness with me when we return to the US.

Odd Things British People Say
About Americans

Back when I first started writing this column (and not long after moving here to the UK), I wrote a post about things British people thought were true of Americans. Needless to say, over the past two years, I've had an opportunity to observe conversations and participate in chats about the British people's views of Americans and thought I'd share a few more of these. This is not meant to be judgmental in any way. I know many Americans who have very false ideas about what Great Britain is like so I think many of these misconceptions go both ways.

That I must really miss living in America. This is probably the most common thing I'm asked about. The truth is, while I really miss my family and close friends, I actually don't miss living in America all that much. Yes, there are plenty of aspects of American culture I miss (My current homesickness symptom is March Madness basketball!), but that comes and goes in brief waves. Overall, I quite like living here.

Most of us shop Black Friday sales. This is a pet peeve of mine, to be completely up front. I'm not a big shopper. I don't really miss shopping in the US (although I definitely made a few Target runs when I was home last summer), and I certainly do not participate in the Black Friday madness. In fact, I don't really personally know that many people who do shop on Black Friday.

But Black Friday has recently become a "thing" here too, with some stores having big sales that day. I was once asked if I was homesick for Black Friday. Not if I was homesick for Thanksgiving. It was so strange.

Americans have a can-do spirit. I had a wonderful conversation with a British man who spent some time living in the US for his job. He loved his time in America, and was very complimentary of our positive outlook. He said, "Americans will get right down to it and work on how to accomplish a task. Brits will just sit around telling you all the reasons you can't do something." I think this is a huge over-generalization, and I find many British people to be very optimistic and hard working. (And there are plenty of Americans who don't fit his description.) But I have to admit, I did appreciate his complimentary take on the US (because sometimes that's not all that common).

Do you own a gun? My husband and I are asked this all the time. I don't want to get into a political debate, but the answer is no. I absolutely love the lack of guns in this culture and I'll miss it greatly when we return to the US.

We like everything to be big. Houses, yards, food portions, cars, parties, etc. In some ways, this is true. The average home in the US is bigger. The food portions are sometimes bigger. (But I think Brits watch a lot of Adam Richman food shows, and think his food eating challenges must be the norm. They're not. You can get reasonable portions at many American restaurants. It's not all steaks the size of your head.)

And certainly, many Americans drive SUVs but the English town I live in seems to have as many enormous Land Rovers as it does small cars, so I certainly don't think a desire for big cars is unique to America. I was chatting with a neighbor about our upcoming village festival and she said, "You probably won't like it. It's nothing like the parties you have in America." I hate that she thought an American wouldn't enjoy an event like that just because it wasn't some flashy big production.

Our Quaint Village Newsletter

One of the most unexpected joys of living in England has been discovering how much we love living in our small, beautiful village. I thought I'd feel so isolated living in such a place, but instead it feels so much like home.

I always love when I walk through my door and see that our monthly village newsletter has arrived through the mail slot while I was gone. It's full of calendar items and other items of interest and is distinctly English in every way. I thought it would be fun to share a bit about its typical content for those of you who are curious as to what life in a small English village is really like.

Seasonal Photos.

The cover is almost always a photo (taken by various villagers who submit them to the "editor") of the village in that particular season. For example, our current June newsletter is a photo from the first May bank holiday celebration at our village pub, with lots of villagers wrapping ribbons around the May Pole. Other times, its scenes of the countryside in our village, like bluebells in bloom or the autumn leaves changing color in fall.

Advertisements for Local Businesses

In my small village, there are relatively few businesses. But they all advertise in our village newsletter. Most notable is our village pub's monthly ad, because it usually lists upcoming special events at the pub, or special deals or takeaway offers.

This is how I find out about things like the Halloween party they hosted for kids, or the 2 for £15 fish n' chip takeaway special on Wednesday evenings. There's usual ads for a local roofer, real estate agent, accountant, handyman and chimney sweep, too. Sometimes individuals run ads, too. I found an occasional babysitter for my children through our village newsletter.

Parish Council Update

There's always an update from our parish council. That's our local government body in our village. (Towns have town councils; cities have city councils). More often than not, the update is usually a request for more people from the village to serve on the council. Currently, only 5 of the 7 seats in our council are filled. Officially our councilors are "elected" although I don't think there's much competition! Otherwise, the update is usually just a brief synopsis of previous council meetings. I want to make it a goal to attend a meeting before we move away, as I think it would be interesting to see the village government first-hand. Sometimes our area's MP (member of parliament) submits a brief report of any important local issues.

Crime Report

The county police department submits a record of any crime reports in our village. Typically, there aren't any, which is wonderful. Occasionally there's a report of a car theft, but that's about it.

Bus Timetable

This is a somewhat new component to the newsletter. When I first moved here, there was no real public transport option in and out of my village. But over the past year, we now have bus service to various towns 4 days per week (it goes to different towns each day). We're fortunate to have two cars in our family so I don't need to rely on this service, but it's nice to know it's there should we ever need it.

Church News

Our village church always provides updates in the newsletter also. Usually the priest writes a letter, along with the schedule of upcoming church services. Our village church shares a priest with several other nearby village churches. (And yes, our village has a church, otherwise it wouldn't be considered a village at all!)

Village Shop Update

One unique aspect of our village is that we have a nonprofit corner shop, run entirely by volunteers from the village. (Many villages have a small shop, but it's usually a for-profit entity.) Their contribution to the newsletter usually includes a request for volunteers, any seasonal produce on offer, the opening/closing times, and other special news, like pre-ordering food for holidays.

Village Sports Updates

Our village pub has several sports teams, including a darts team and pétanque teams. (I'll have to write a future post about pétanque as I'm still learning about it!)

The sports update usually includes information on how the nearby rugby and football teams and clubs are faring also, as our village is far too small to have its own.

Rubbish Information

No, I don't mean the information in our newsletter is rubbish! As I've explained in a previous post, our rubbish bins are collected every other week, and on the non-collection week, our recycling is collected instead. So the newsletter always has that schedule, as it's easy to forget which week is which. This is the single most important reason I always keep our newsletter!

My First Dentist Appointment in England

I had somehow managed to avoid going to the dentist since moving to England. I always just made an appointment with a dentist while visiting the States. But I decided that I didn't want to waste some of my precious time "home" this summer at the dentist's office, so I finally booked an appointment with a dentist here. I could tell from the moment I made the appointment that there would be both similarities and differences between the UK and America.

(Also, please note, I can only speak from the experience of the dentists I've seen in the US, and the one I have seen here in the UK. I know there is probably a great deal of variation across the two countries. I'm not intending for this to be an all-knowing post. It merely reflects the very individual experience I had.)

Similarities:

The Office

If you had walked into the office here in England, you might have guessed you were in a dentist office in the US. Waiting room, receptionist, the same reclining mechanical chairs, and the lamp that hangs overhead. There were signs and posters up about proper dental care, etc. If I didn't know that the exterior of the building dates back to the 16th century, I might have thought I was back in America.

The Tools

These were quite similar as well. The metal pick that they use to clean the plaque off your teeth, the polishing tool, even the x-ray experience was the same, as I had to bite down on those boards they put in your mouth.

Cost

When I called to make the appointment, they told me there was a long wait for NHS appointments, or I could pay on my own and get in right away. I chose to visit right away, as I was trying to get it done before my kids were off from school for the summer. I had to pay out of pocket for the past couple of dental appointments anyway, since I didn't have dental coverage when we were visiting the US. I can't remember exactly what I paid in the U.S, but I'm pretty sure it was roughly to similar to the cost here. I assume if I had waited for an NHS appointment, it would have been free or relatively low cost, much like those with dental insurance in the US experience.

Differences:

Scheduling Process

When I called, the receptionist asked if I wanted to see a hygienist or a dentist. I said preferably both, but that I mostly just wanted to get my teeth cleaned. (I've never had dental problems in the past and wasn't concerned about anything this time around, either.) She explained that to see the hygienist, I first had to book an appointment with a dentist who would then "prescribe" me a visit to the hygienist.

In my experience in the US, I've always had my teeth cleaned by a hygienist first, and then the dentist checks you out. Regardless, the receptionist was able to book me back-to-back appointments, so the flow of the visit was relatively seamless. I did see the dentist first, and then he passed me along to the hygienist for cleaning after a brief wait.

Length of Time

I was in and out in under 30 minutes. This included 10 minutes spent in the waiting room. I spent a short amount of time with the dentist, which didn't surprise me a bit. What did surprise me is that it only took the hygienist 12 minutes to clean my teeth. This included at least a few minutes of chatting and discussing my next appointment. I was shocked at how quickly the cleaning was.

Thoroughness of the Cleaning

I really wanted the visit to go well. I know the stereotype that perhaps dental care here isn't quite up to par with the US, but I really didn't buy into that at all. However, after having experienced a cleaning here, I'm not sure I'd do it again. I'd prefer to pay to have my teeth cleaned in the US. I love that smooth, squeaky clean feeling I get after a cleaning that lasts for at least a few days after my US dental visits. I walked out of this visit without that feeling whatsoever. It truly felt like I had just brushed my teeth well, not that professional feeling at all. The fact that the cleaning only lasted about 10 minutes was pretty disappointing.

Number of Staff

There was an assistant helping the dentist, and an assistant helping the hygienist. It seemed a bit much for four people to be hovering over me over the course of the visit. I was actually relieved when I saw the bill, as I figured with that much staff tending to me, I might be charged more than I was expecting based on US costs.

Going forward, I'm debating what to do about my children. They're both very due for a cleaning (although fortunately they both still only have baby teeth).

I don't want to waste time when we could be visiting with friends and family this summer during our visit to the US, but I also felt like my visit to the dentist here was a bit of a waste. That said, if we were to have any kind of serious dental trouble here, I'm quite confident in the skills of the dentist I saw. He was very professional and the office seemed to have quality equipment.

Having a Great British Summer

I've always loved summer, but perhaps never more so than when I moved to England two years ago. As I'm entering my third summer, and possibly my last, I'm reflecting on why a Great British Summer really is so great.

Wimbledon

Before I moved here, I had the impression that life in the UK must come to a grinding halt during Wimbledon. I assumed it was the UK equivalent of the American Super Bowl. To be fair, it is a big deal, and it's on television for two straight weeks. However, it doesn't attract quite the hoopla or extravagance that some big American sporting events do. (That's probably a testament to cultural differences more than anything.) Regardless, I love it. It just seems so classically British, and my family has enjoyed embracing Andy Murray as our new favorite player. He won the tournament our first summer, which only added to the excitement that year.

Strawberries

Speaking of Wimbledon, where the trademark food is strawberries and cream, I love the strawberries here. Maybe it's just in my head, but I swear they taste better than American strawberries. There are several memories of strawberries I'll take with me from our time here.

First, there's a beautiful u-pick strawberry patch just 15 minutes from my house. Each summer, I've taken my kids there to pick strawberries and it's always one of our favorite outings.

I've also become a huge fan of the British dessert Eton Mess. If you've never tried it, be sure to do so on your next trip over (or make it yourself). I'll be whipping up a batch with the strawberries we picked this week on Sunday while we watch the Wimbledon finals.

Pimm's

Another British summer staple is a cold glass of Pimm's with lemonade. And by lemonade, I don't mean the American style lemonade. Lemonade here is a lemon-flavored soda (somewhat comparable to Sprite). Pimm's is a liqueur, often served with lemonade and strawberries, cucumber, mint, etc. I always make it for guests or force them to order it out at a pub when they're here, and inevitably they buy some at the duty free shop on their way back to the US. It's refreshing, quenches your thirst, and is just a great summer drink.

Everything is Open

One thing that surprised me when we moved here is that many visitor attractions shut down in the colder months or have greatly reduced hours. Sometimes this means we can't show favorite places off to people who visit us in the autumn, winter or spring. And I'm always a little disappointed when I get an idea for a weekend outing for my family, only to realize we'll have to delay visiting until June when it re-opens for the year. But in the summer, everything opens back up and we are spoiled for options of places to visit around the country. Weekends are full of festivals, village fetes, and other big events. There's just so much going on at this time of year, while it can sometimes feel a bit sleepy in the winter.

Weather

Everyone loves to moan about the weather in the UK, but I find it quite mild, typically. The summer can sometimes still be wet and cold, but more often than not, we have beautiful days. I'm from the Midwest, where July and August can sometimes be brutally hot and have us stuck inside in our air conditioned homes. Not here! I love nothing more than to open the doors to my back garden and let my sons run in and out of the house all day long throughout the summer.

The Beach

Because it's an island, most Brits are never more than a few hours' drive from a beautiful beach. My family adores going to Brancaster Beach in Norfolk on the weekends as a day trip, and it's one of the things I'll miss when I return to America and am once again a 12-hour drive from the closest beach.

Digging into My English Town's History

One of the things I most enjoy about living in Europe is the love and appreciation of history here. There is a real desire to preserve, remember and reflect on each country and region's past. It's obvious to visitors, just in the way that so many buildings are kept up instead of knocked down.

I mentioned in a post that I wrote about antique shopping here that I picked up a book about the town I live in that dates back to 1936. I thought it would be interesting to dig inside its pages and see how much is the same here, and how much has changed.

On the cover of the book is a drawing of the view of the town as you come in via a particular street. I'm stunned at how little has changed.

The welcome letter at the front of the book praises the town's stone buildings and interesting architecture, its quality education, and its robust shopping for a town of its size. Stamford often ranks highly today as one of the best places to live in the UK, and it's for these exact same reasons it often earns this designation.

One photo from the book that jumped out at me is a view of the Meadows. This is an area of town that is quite active these days with dog walkers, children playing, ice cream vans, festivals, etc.

But in 1936, there's a photo with cows grazing! I often park near here, and always wondered why that parking area is referred to as the "Cattle Market" car park. Now I understand!

All major churches described in the book are still standing and landmarks in the town today. However, in 1936 they appear to be the hub of the town's activity and that no longer seems to be the case today, or at least not in the way they once were.

There is a mention in the book that there are about a half dozen roads that converge upon the town. I wouldn't venture to guess how many roads come into the town today, but certainly more than 6!

The local park is described in the book, and for the most part, the park today is exactly as described, including tennis courts, a playground, and open green space. And still in the same location and still called by the same name. However, a couple of years ago a skate park was added. Something I'm guessing they could have never imagined in 1936!

There is a portion of the book that lists the 5 principal hotels in town. Two are still in operation at the same locations. Both would definitely still be considered two of the principal hotels today.

A few of the advertisements stood out to me as well. One was an ad for Central Restaurant, which still exists today serving basically the same food mentioned in 1936! There was an ad for Boots, a chain pharmacy that I had no idea dated that far back. (It's still in the same location as advertised then, with the same logo!) The town newspaper,

Stamford Mercury, ran an ad in the book and is also still in operation.

The village I live in, which lies just outside the town limits, is also described in an article describing various nearby villages. It mentions that the village has an old sundial that may still be seen in a garden, as a relic of a former palace here. I'm proud to say that the sundial has now been restored and I peek in on it often as I walk through my village. A perfect example of the emphasis on preservation here.

This book was such a fascinating look into a time long gone in my town's history, and it was also somehow comforting that some things really do stay the same.

Funny Things My Expat Kids Have Said Since Moving to the UK

Remember that Bill Cosby show "Kids Say the Darndest Things"? I think it was on back in the 90s and featured funny videos of kids saying hilarious things. I love the fact that young children have no filter, and say whatever is on their mind. Over the past year, I've observed my 5-year-old saying some pretty funny or interesting things about moving to a new country that I thought I'd share.

When will I start talking differently?

He said this as we walked off the airplane when we landed at Heathrow on our first day living in the UK. Perhaps we had over-prepared him for the changes in accent that happen when you move from America to the UK, as he thought it would be immediate. The best part was listening to our fellow passengers chuckle at this question.

Should I color this ambulance English or American?

We were coloring pictures from a coloring book together, and his picture was of an ambulance. The ambulances around our house here in the East Midlands are bright green, whereas the ambulances he was used to seeing in the US were white or red.

One of the greatest reasons it's so fun to move abroad with young children is that they notice things you don't. I'm certain it wouldn't have occurred to me to point out this sort of difference.

Mom, you know that's not the proper way to count, right?

I was counting to ten out loud on my fingers, starting with my index finger as is customary in the US. However, he had already noticed that his teacher at school starts with her thumb. This is one of his favorite cultural differences. Go ahead and give it a try: we've decided that the number 4 is easier the US way, but the number 3 is easier the British way.

Mom, you can speak American to me. I still remember American even though I speak English now.

He said this to me as he was getting dressed for school one morning. I happened to call his sweater a jumper, as they do here, but he was more accustomed to me calling it a sweater and wondered why I was using the British word for it. (I should also note that he uses the word "English" and "British" pretty interchangeably right now, and doesn't completely understand the difference between the two. Although he does know which is the English flag and which is the British flag.)

Remember to say "wad-ur, " not "wat-uh. "

This one is my favorite. Of all the words that my children now say with a British accent, the difference in "water" is most drastic. And it is also the first word we noticed that they both started saying with a British accent after we moved here.

So when we visited the US this summer, the first thing my 5-year-old said to his 2-year-old brother was to remind him how Americans say "water. "

I've been keeping detailed notes on the transformation in the way my children speak, and at some point, I'll write a post about their progression toward a British accent. It's probably clear just from this post that they are well on their way toward sounding fully British!

School

A British School Uniform

My oldest child starts school this week. He's four, which means in the US he would have attended preschool for a few hours each week this year. But in Great Britain, school begins at four, and thus I sent him on his way to "Reception" (what Americans call Kindergarten).

Like any mom, I spent the last few weeks in preparation for school by learning the components of a British school uniform. All schoolchildren here, from what I can tell, wear a uniform of some kind. My son's school has a very complex uniform, including three separate "official" bags (books, gym clothes, and swim gear). A big change for a mom used to shipping him off to preschool in a t-shirt and shorts most days!

So here are the basic elements of his uniform this year:

A Blazer

It's hard to imagine my 4-year-old wearing a blazer. He didn't even wear a jacket when he was a ring bearer in a wedding! And yet off he goes each morning in it. From what I'm told, the children remove them pretty quickly once arriving in their classroom so it doesn't get dirty. Which I'm thankful for, since it was quite expensive.

A Jumper

What most Americans would call a sweater. My son's is V-neck with the school emblem. I suspect he'll wear it daily once the weather cools.

Polo Shirts

He has both short-sleeve and long-sleeve as an option each day, in red. In future years, he'll switch to a more formal dress shirt and tie.

Shorts or Trousers

I love the look of little boys in knee-high socks and dress shorts. We just need to remember to call the "pants" trousers!

A Cap

He wears a wool cap with the school emblem each day. Because they spend a lot of time outdoors at his school, he also has a sunhat, which looks like a baseball cap with flaps.

School Shoes

A black pair of school shoes is a pretty universal clothing item for all British school children. Every shoe store has an entire rack devoted to these classic shoes.

That sums up his day-to-day look. Like I mentioned, he also has several bags, a gym outfit (shorts and a white polo shirt), attire for swimming (trunks and a swim cap), and soon we'll add winter gear like coats, hats, scarves and gloves to the mix.

And while I'm definitely in favor of the uniform (No fights about wearing the same superhero shirt each morning!), I was not a fan of having to sew in name labels on each of these items, even the socks.

I purchased most of this, particularly those items with the school emblem, at his school's supply store. The more basic pieces I was able to get at John Lewis, a popular department store here. You'll find school uniform pieces being sold at most stores, even grocery stores.

I realize not every child's uniform across the country looks just like this. But this has been our experience adjusting to a new code of dress.

British Things My 4-Year-Old Says

One of the things we wondered about when we moved to England was how long it would take our children to acclimatize to the way of life here. Naturally, this includes the different accent and the many uniquely British sayings. We've been shocked by how quickly our oldest, who is 4 years old and attends a British school full-time, has picked up on all of it. In fact, he now speaks with more than just a hint of a British accent.

I've been keeping track of the progression as it happens, so at some point a year or two from now, I'll share how the transformation in the way he speaks went. But for now, I thought it would be fun to list a few of the British things he says regularly.

The Loo

Naturally, at 4, habits relating to what he previously called "the potty" come up in conversation a lot. I think after only about two weeks in school, I would hear him saying "the loo" or "the toilet" instead of bathroom or potty.

Easy Peasy

I had heard this expression from time to time in the US, used whenever something is easy to do, but it's much more common here, and I now catch my son saying it all the time. If I ask him to help with something, he'll often reply, "Sure, that'll be easy peasy." Or, "Look Mom, this is easy peasy!"

Ready, steady, go!

In the US, to start a race you'd probably say, "Ready, set, go." But here, it's "Ready, steady, go." It was further ingrained in my son's vocabulary because the popular children's television network here, called CBeebies, has a song that comes on in between shows that includes the lyrics, "Ready, steady, get set, go" over and over.

This will take ages.

This expression always makes me laugh, especially coming from a 4-year-old. To an American like me, it seems so dramatic and old-fashioned. He says it all the time, like when we're waiting at a red light, talking about the upcoming Christmas holiday, or even waiting 15 more minutes for my husband to get home from work so we can eat dinner as a family.

Tidy Up

One of the funniest conversations I've ever had with him happened during his first week of school. I asked him what he liked best about school, and he said, "When it's time to tidy up." I laughed and asked why he never liked cleaning up at home, but liked it so much at school. He said, "Well, Mom, you say clean up and at school they say tidy up. I only like to tidy up." From that point on, we've called it tidy up!

Nearly. Instead of saying "almost" he now says "nearly" instead. As in, "Mom, I'm nearly ready for school." Or "I'm nearly done looking at this book."

Some of these differences probably seem quite subtle, but they're pretty eye-opening to a parent. It's been really fun to watch the transformation in him since he started school, and language development and differences are a big part of that.

Differences in Parenting between America and Britain

I'm a little hesitant to write this post, as I know making any sort of commentary about parenting approaches is like opening a gigantic can of worms. I will make some generalizations in this post that I know are not true for every family or every parent, and I realize my thoughts and opinions on parenting are not shared by everyone. I wouldn't expect that to be the case, and I embrace that. But I thought addressing some of the differences I've noticed in parenting styles between the US and Great Britain was an interesting topic, and something I've spent a lot of time observing over the past 9 months since moving to England.

In general, I feel as though British parents seem to be less "helicopter."

This is by and large the biggest difference I've noticed, and for the most part I think it's great. At the playground, in the school yard, even just walking around town, I notice that parents hover much less than American parents. They don't seem quick to get involved in some of the little squabbles that develop between young children, instead letting the kids sort it out for themselves. And I find parents here to be much more encouraging of children taking risks (but safely!) at places like playgrounds. I think it leads directly to my next observation:

British children are encouraged to be more independent at an earlier age.

At the parent meeting we attended in the summer, during the weeks leading up to our 4-year-old starting school, we were encouraged to make sure our son could cut his own food and dress himself completely on his own. This came as a bit of a shock to us... he hadn't mastered either skill, and I knew of few kids his age in the US who could do these things at such a young age. But sure enough, he's picked it up quite quickly and can now do both. He's now expected to keep track of all his belongings at school, get his homework done, etc. I've heard from fellow expats living here with older kids that this will continue on into his school years. I'm excited to see this develop in him, as I think in America we tend to "baby" our children well into their school years (not that there is anything wrong with that either, but it's been fun to see him come into his own a bit since we moved here).

British children begin school at a younger age.

Yes, school starts at 4 years of age here with reception (roughly equivalent to the US kindergarten, which typically begins at age 5 or 6). But it's common to begin placing children in nursery (equivalent to US preschool) as early as 1. Beginning at age 3 in the UK, families are entitled to 15 hours per week of government-funded nursery/preschool. In the US, some kids don't set foot in a school setting until Pre-K (age 4-5), and even then, it's often only for a few hours each week, as the cost is typically on the shoulders of families.

Napping seems to be less of a priority here.

This is very much anecdotal, just what I've noticed on a personal level. In the US, I feel as though parents of young children place a big emphasis on napping, and ensuring that young children take a good nap each day. Here, I often notice toddlers out and about in the middle of the afternoon (when my own 2-year-old is sound asleep each day). Toddler groups and classes often meet in the afternoons, whereas in the US those were typically limited to mornings or early evenings. People here are sometimes shocked when I say that my 4-year-old was still regularly napping until he started school this fall. I'm not saying British kids don't nap, I'm certain that they do. But it just seems less routine here than in the US.

There is a greater emphasis on outdoor play.

I'm a huge believer in the benefits of children playing and spending a lot of time outdoors, so I'm glad it's a priority here as well. Every school we toured prior to moving (both private and public) had a classroom style that allowed a lot of indoor/outdoor movement. My son spends a large portion of his school day outdoors, regardless of weather conditions. In the US, outdoor time is often restricted just to recess. Even cultural attractions, like National Trust properties, spend a lot of their resources maintaining and encouraging families to use outdoor spaces, like adventure playgrounds, bike trails, hiking paths, nature workshops, etc.

It's impossible to articulate an entire country's parenting philosophy in under 800 words, nor do I know enough about that to do so. That's definitely not my intention in writing this post. Again, this is just my very unscientific observations regarding some general differences in parenting between the US and the UK.

My Kids' Favorite British Children's Book Authors

My family is preparing for a visit back to the US this summer. I've been thinking about what to pack that will entertain my children on the long flight back, and what struck me is how different my children's tastes are in toys and books since we moved here. For the most part, they are no longer interested in the Elmo videos and PBS Kids apps, or the books based on various Nick Jr. characters that long dominated their hearts when we lived in America. They've been replaced by countless equally-as-loved characters from British cartoons and literature. Here are a few of their favorites.

Julia Donaldson

A friend introduced my family to the popular children's book *The Gruffalo* by Julia Donaldson before we moved here because she knew it was popular here. That friend was so right! Everywhere you look here, especially at child-friendly places, is *The Gruffalo*. It's a charming book and my kids love it. Donaldson has also written a few other books my children really enjoy, like *Room on the Broom* and *What the Ladybird Heard*.

Judith Kerr

Not originally from Great Britain, Kerr's family fled Germany during WWII. Her most popular titles are a series of books based on a cat called Mog and *The Tiger Who Came to Tea*.

I think what I like best about these books is that there is no mistaking their British roots. When the tiger comes to tea, it's not just for the drink, as most Americans would believe. Tea can also mean a meal served in the late afternoon or early evening, and that's just what the tiger is after. And the mother and father in the Mog series are often heard saying, "Bother that cat!" Bother in this instance being a uniquely British saying, similar to the way "darn" would be used in America.

Lauren Child

My oldest son was introduced to a series of books based on characters named Charlie and Lola when he began school. We have eagerly embraced Charlie and Lola into our lives since then. Child's writing is funny and down-to-earth, and Charlie and Lola are very fun characters. (They've also been turned into a hit children's television show.) If you've got plans to bring your children across the pond for a stay in London anytime soon, the book *Charlie and Lola: We Completely Must Go to London* would be a great read.

Roger Hargreaves

I distinctly remember a stack of books at my children's library growing up, small, square and white, each based on a different character: "Mr. Happy, " "Little Miss Cheerful, " "Mr. Strong, " "Little Miss Sunshine, " etc. Turns out, it is a series of books called *Mr. Men* by Hargreaves. And while the series dates back to the 1970s, it is back in a big way here across the pond, with a popular television show to boot. My oldest can't get enough of these fun stories.

I look forward to my children getting a bit older, so that I can introduce them to some of my other favorite British children's book authors, like J.K. Rowling and the *Harry Potter* series, or Roald Dahl, author of *Charlie and the Chocolate Factory* and *James and the Giant Peach*, among many others. Who are your favorite British children's book authors?

British Words Every Parent of Young Children Learns

A really great friend of mine just moved over to the UK with her young children. Our husbands work for the same company, and I feel very fortunate to have a friend from "home" joining me in this adventure. Naturally I've been answering lots of questions for her, just as I asked what felt like thousands of questions of fellow expats, neighbors and even strangers when I first moved here.

One of the things I've had to learn, among many other things, is new terminology, phrases and activities that are unique to my particular stage of life: a parent of young children. I'm sure I'd be learning all about A Levels and GCSEs if my kids were older. So these are some things I'll share with my friend who is new to life here, as she helps her young children navigate a new way of living.

Den Building

I remember seeing this advertised in brochures on attractions which offered "den building" activities for kids. When I think of a den, I think of something a bear lives in. Or perhaps an old-fashioned word for living room. But in this instance, a den is a little hut made of long sticks that children enjoy building in the woods. (It's shaped like a pyramid, and looks almost like a teepee.) I've mentioned before that I think there is a huge emphasis here in the UK on getting children outdoors and playing creatively, which I love.

Den building is just one of the ways kids are enticed to explore their natural surroundings. My own boys now enjoy building dens when we go on hikes in the woods (or playing in those they find along the way built by other children.) The tricky thing is, I'm not sure what this sort of structure would be called in America!

Fancy Dress

I stumbled upon this one on an invitation to a child's birthday party. I wrongly thought this meant my son needed to be dressed as if he were going to a wedding. Luckily I realized my mistake before I sent him off to the party in a suit and tie. Instead, fancy dress means a costume. Like a super hero, pirate or princess.

Discos

When my son's school held a disco one afternoon after school as a fundraiser, I had visions of John Travolta in *Saturday Night Fever*, but it's really just a dance.

Tuck Shop

I sent my son off to a little day camp a few weeks after we moved here. When I got the paperwork the week before camp explaining what would take place, they encouraged parents to send some money with their child to use in the tuck shop. I had absolutely no clue what a tuck shop was. Fortunately, Google saved the day, as it often does for me, and I learned that a tuck shop is simply just a place where kids can buy a little treat or snack or drink (usually used in a school-like setting).

Pocket money. Whereas in the US you might refer to money you give your children as an allowance or spending money, here it's called pocket money. It's just a little amount that can be used to spend as they see fit. Even our teenage babysitter refers to her earnings as pocket money.

Now if the school tells me to send some pocket money with my son to use at the tuck shop during the disco, I know exactly what's going on!

Differences in Primary School Between the UK and USA

My children went back to school last week, as did many children in the US and UK. This is now our third year sending my oldest (6 years old) to a British school, and it seems worthy of a few posts explaining some of the differences I've observed between primary schools in the UK and elementary schools in the US.

A few things to point out initially: my son attends a private school here in England. This is the only school from which I have first-hand information and experience (understandably). And my son was not old enough to attend school in the US (other than preschool) prior to my family moving abroad, so the only knowledge I have of elementary school in the US is my own education and my niece's, nephew's and friends' presently, all of which are from public schools. I am quite aware that schools vary across the country, and even from town to town, so my observations of differences might not align with what readers might be familiar with from schools in the UK and US.

Uniform

I've written a pretty thorough explanation of my son's uniform for Anglotopia. From my observation, in my part of England, all students wear uniforms to primary school. I'm not aware of any primary schools near my house who do not.

Yet in the US, this isn't quite as a common, and certainly not as common at public schools. I like to show my son photos of his friends and family back in America on their first day of school, and he is always startled a bit at first to see children dressed so casually for school. I have to say, I love the uniform because it means we don't have to figure out what he's going to wear each day. Plus, I think he looks so cute in his knee socks, blazer and cap.

Age School Begins

This was the biggest difference for me to adjust to when we moved here, mostly because it affected my family so much. Full-time school begins at age 4 here (or the school year in which you turn 5). This is a full year earlier than kindergarten begins in the US. As my son was 4 the summer we moved, he began school that fall, even though in the US he would have gone to preschool that year.

This early start to school is different from some other European countries and is often debated here in the UK. Overall, I was pleased with my son's experience that first year, but he was extremely exhausted in the evenings and often took long naps on the weekend to catch up on his rest.

Terminology

In the US, what we would call a school principal is called the head teacher. And the term for grade levels is different also. The first year of school is called Reception (when you are age 4-5, as mentioned above).

It is then called Year 1, Year 2, Year 3, etc. For example, my son is in Year 2, which is called First Grade in the US. School holidays/vacations are referred to differently (half-term breaks in October and March instead of Fall Break and Spring Break).

Outdoor Play Time

I find my son has much more outdoor playtime (or recess, as it's called in the US) than his American counterparts. Again, I'm sure this varies from school to school, but he gets a 15-minute play break in the morning, a much longer break after he eats lunch (30-45 minutes, typically), and then another 15 minutes in the afternoon. This is in addition to any outdoor learning time that might be built into the day. His school day is slightly longer than what I understand the average day in the US to be (he begins at 8:20 and ends at 3:45), but I know this varies drastically from school to school in both countries.

Assembly

His entire school gathers for "assembly" at least two days each week. Sometimes it's just for the head teacher to make announcements or hand out awards, other times they have a special speaker or students might perform. I find these school-wide gatherings happen far less often in the US, but again, this is a difference that's probably unique to each school, not necessarily country to country.

Food at School

The first difference to note is that they call lunch "dinner" at his school. He's also provided with a snack in the morning (usually an apple, pear or banana) and the afternoon (typically a biscuit, similar to a graham cracker in the US). As the students in his school get older, they bring their own snack into school.

Again, I realize I can't speak for all British schools and all American schools. Perhaps your son or daughter attends an American school and wears a uniform and plays outside all day, but these are just a few general differences I've observed. Overall, my son has received a fantastic education here and we love his school, but I'm sure we'll also settle back into the swing of things in the American school system when the time comes.

A Guide to English School Dinner

Last month, I wrote about a few differences and observations I've made about primary school here (or, at least my son's experience). One of the biggest differences is how the children are fed at my son's school. I'm sure this differs greatly around the country.

First, my son eats three times throughout the day at school. In the morning, he's offered apples, pears or bananas as a snack. In the afternoon, he's given a biscuit (similar to an American graham cracker) as a snack. Children who are older are allowed to bring in their own snack.

But the main meal is served around noon and called dinner. The biggest cultural difference for me as a parent is that I'm not allowed to pack him a lunch, he must eat what's served at school. One of the best examples of how being an expat and adjusting to a new way of life can be so beneficial is the change in how I feel about this rule. When he first began school, I was really upset about this policy. I worried he wouldn't eat much of the food and be hungry all day.

Now, I'm the biggest believer in this policy. He eats a relatively healthy, hot meal each day. He's become much more willing to try new foods, and there's a much greater variety in the foods he enjoys. And on the days where he doesn't like it? He forces himself to eat just enough to get by. Which is fine with me.

So what does he eat? Here's the menu this week at school. (There's also a vegetarian option but he rarely chooses that, so I feel like I can't speak to that with much first-hand knowledge.)

Monday: Pasta with tomato sauce or cheese sauce and a salad
Tuesday: Cottage pie with mixed vegetables
Wednesday: Roasted gammon (ham) with pineapple, roast potatoes, carrots and peas
Thursday: Chicken Kiev with new potatoes and sweetcorn
Friday: Sausage, chips, and baked beans or cucumbers

In general, Wednesdays are almost always "roast dinner" days, where the children are served what would traditionally be served as a Sunday roast dinner. Fridays are almost always either fish and chips or sausage and chips. But the menu the rest of the week varies greatly and has a lot of variety.

Because all children eat what's served by the school, there is no need to have a nut-free table as many schools in the US have. It is an entirely nut-free school. Since my son is allergic to tree nuts, it's such a relief to know he won't be exposed to nuts while eating at school. If students have other allergies (dairy, etc.), the staff have alternative meals available to them.

As for the cafeteria, it looks very similar to any school cafeteria I've seen in the US. He lines up, grabs a tray, is served by the kitchen staff (he calls them dinner ladies), and then sits down.

He eats his main meal, and when he has finished or feels done, he raises his hand and a staff member comes around, looks to see how much he has had to eat, and then allows him to eat his pudding (dessert). They can also choose a piece of fruit as their pudding. Once they have finished their pudding, they can go outside to play for the remainder of the hour-long lunch period. Pudding is usually some type of cake.

Another observation? All children eat with a knife and fork. The staff assist the very young children to cut their food, but for the most part, the children, beginning at age 4, do this independently. I love that they are also expected to demonstrate appropriate table manners.

Most of all, after a summer of making my boys sandwiches every day, I'm just glad I never have to pack him a lunch!

Travelogues

Following in Paddington Bear's Shoes in London: A Paddington Tour of London

Since the movie was released here in the UK in late November, Paddington Bear has been all the rage (at least among young children, the segment of the population I'm most familiar with!). Last month, my family thoroughly enjoyed a trip to the cinema to see the film (as you'd say here). I've always adored the books, but it was so fun to see the story come to life on the big screen. I hope Paddington's newfound popularity lasts for a long time.

I think my favorite aspect of the movie, though, was seeing some of my favorite places in London featured so prominently in the movie. Indeed, a few days later we took a day trip into the city and saw several of the Paddington statues that were set up as part of the Paddington Trail. Unfortunately, that was a temporary exhibition and most of the statues have now been taken down. But I thought it might be fun to put together a list of London attractions closely connected to the story of Paddington Bear.

Paddington Station

You should begin where Paddington began his London adventures. He arrived on a train in Paddington Station and waited on the platform until the Brown family offered their help.

While not particularly worth a trip just to see the station (unless you love train stations), you can catch a train to Windsor, Bath and Oxford, among other places, for a fun day trip outside the city. Or just plan to take the Heathrow Express into or out of the city to catch your flight. At 30 minutes, it's the quickest way to the airport from London's city center.

Portobello Road Market

In the movie, Mrs. Brown takes Paddington to an antique shop along Portobello Road to identify the origin of his famous red hat. Mr. Gruber's Antique Store is actually Alice's Antiques, located at 86 Portobello Road. The entire stretch of Portobello Road is a lively market each Saturday, with an enormous selection of antiques and collectables.

Buckingham Palace

In many of the promotional pictures for the film, Paddington is standing in front of Buckingham Palace. While he doesn't spend much time there in the movie, there is one memorable and heartwarming scene with this famous backdrop. I just don't advise you try to stand right next to one of the guards as he does.

Marmalade Sandwiches

Everyone knows that Paddington survives on marmalade sandwiches. Fancy trying one yourself? Head to **Borough Market**, one of my favorite spots in the city.

You'll be surrounded by delicious food, as this is the largest food market in the city. The market's website outlines where you can pick up all the ingredients you'll need to recreate Paddington's favorite food: Borough Market's Ultimate Marmalade Sandwich. But if you'd rather just pick up a jar of orange marmalade to bring home, then I'd recommend **Fortnum & Mason**, one of London's oldest and most prestigious stores. They sell an amazing array of British food products.

Natural History Museum

I don't want to give away any details, but in the movie Paddington's darkest hour takes place in the Natural History Museum. Fortunately, there's a happy ending, and so you won't find a stuffed Peruvian bear in the museum. The Natural History Museum is largely considered to be one of London's top museums. The gorgeous building alone makes it worth the trip.

Shopping

No Paddington adventure would be complete without a souvenir. Hamleys, London's premiere toy shop, has a huge selection of Paddington Bear toys. Here you'll be in the thick of the London shopping scene along Regent Street. Or go where it all began, Selfridges department store, on Oxford Street. The character of Paddington Bear was inspired by a teddy bear purchased at Selfridges by the book's author, Michael Bond, for his wife.

A Perfect Day Out at Rutland Water in the East Midlands

When one conjures up idyllic days spent in England, one might naturally lean toward historic castle visits, afternoon teas, and other calm, indoor pursuits. But I'm quickly learning that the English are an active bunch. And particularly on those most cherished days, when the clouds push off and the sun warms everything up, people here flock to bikes, boats and jogging paths.

A great place to pursue outdoor adventure in England is at Western Europe's largest man-made lake, Rutland Water. Built as a reservoir in 1977, it supplies water to 500,000 people in five neighboring counties.

But while the area might be "new," it doesn't lack interest, even of the historical variety. You'll find 24 miles of path that runs around the perimeter, providing shoreline views throughout along with woodland and pastures. Sheep graze right up to the path and will move out of your way as you breeze by.

There is a great deal of activity both on the water and surrounding the lake. Here is my recommendation for a great day out at Rutland Water.

- Begin your day by renting bikes for a couple of hours at the Rutland Cycling bike hire and shop, located at the Normanton Car Park (postal code LE15 8HD). They've got a wide range of quality bikes, and all sorts of options if you plan to bring kids along.

- A perfect 2-hour route would be to head northwest on the path toward Normanton Church. This church was one of the few sites saved when the reservoir was constructed. It dates back to medieval times, although portions have been reconstructed. It is only open for tours seasonally, so call ahead to 01780 686800. But even if you can't step inside, it's beautiful enough to admire from the outside.

- From Normanton Church, continue cycling along the path to the dam. As you cross the dam, you'll be able to admire the water on your left and the picturesque village of Empingham on your right.

- After you've crossed the dam, you'll come upon the Rutland Visitor's Centre, as well as a quality adventure playground for the kids. Another great spot to take a break and enjoy the water views or some playtime. This stop has amenities such as toilets and snacks.

- We finished the first half of our cycle ride by continuing on to The Harbour Café and marina. Here you can purchase lunch and picnic along the water, or dine indoors and take a break from the elements. From there, we turned around and headed back to the Normanton Car Park to return our bikes. Naturally, we had to get a few ice cream cones at the outdoor café before heading home.

I have no doubt we'll make a return to Rutland Water for a lot of other activities. If you're not into cycling and would prefer a more leisurely experience, than start your visit at the marina and book a ride on the Rutland Belle, a large boat that will take you around the lake. You'll find all the details on the Rutland Water Cruises website.

You can also easily spend hours birdwatching here. The area is famous for being home to thousands of osprey, which are easy to spot April through October. More information about the nature reserve at Rutland Water is here.

You may need a rest after all this fun and adventure. If you don't want to part ways with the spectacular water views, then book a night at the Normanton Park Hotel, just across the path from the Normanton Church. The house-turned-Best Western dates back to the 1800s, and offers two restaurants and a playground. If you're looking for a property that's closer to more amenities, then search for lodging in the nearby towns of Oakham or Stamford. If you're up for roughing it a bit, you could camp at several of the camping areas available around the water.

So when the forecast calls for sun, do what the Brits do, and grab your "sun cream" and head for a day of fun and adventure at Rutland Water.

Exploring the Imperial War Museum Duxford

As the last remaining veterans of World War I and World War II pass on, it seems to be a period of history that we're still grasping to wrap our heads around. If you have an interest in the "Imperial Wars," then you'll want to plan visits to the Imperial War Museums around Great Britain.

My family visited the IWM Duxford, just a few minutes outside of Cambridge, last week. It's a series of buildings (including several converted airplane hangars) at a former Royal Air Force airfield, Duxford. To say I've never seen so many airplanes in one facility would be an understatement. There are more than 200 planes, from the iconic Spitfire to the famously fast Concord. Many are open for the public to step inside and imagine flight in such unique aircraft.

Begin your visit at the Air Space. If you have children, this will be an area of great interest to them. You'll start by exploring the history of flight, including lots of hands-on exhibits to demonstrate everything from how hot air rises to G-forces. Then you'll immerse yourself in planes of every shape and size, including at least a dozen or so that you can step inside and explore on your own. Tours in this area are held frequently throughout the day, so look for signs or inquire if you're interested in a more in-depth experience.

You could easily spend an entire weekend covering every inch of this enormous complex, but if you're limited to just a few hours like we were, my advice would be to then head across the grounds to the American Air Museum. In this modern glass building, you'll find all kinds of information and exhibits about the role the US played in these wars, along with many of the aircraft and tanks used by the US military.

The Battle of Britain exhibit was our next stop, housed in the middle of the complex in a 1917 Belfast hangar. This area had a particular interest to me because it addressed the societal effects of these wars, like what life was like for those living under the threat of air attacks in London and elsewhere. I'm not much of a military history buff, but it's hard not to be moved by the thought of keeping your family safe and calm amid nightly air raids.

A few tips if you're planning a visit:

- Bring a stroller and great walking shoes. The grounds are enormous, and while your children are welcome to walk around each building and explore, tiny legs get very tired between buildings.

- There are cafes that serve both cold and hot food scattered around the facility, although you're also welcome to pack a lunch. There's also an outdoor play area for young children near the Air Space building.

- The museum is a great activity for a rainy day, but bring along your rain jackets and umbrellas for the time you spend outside getting between exhibits.

- The museum, just south of Cambridge, is easily accessible off the M11. It would make a great day trip from both London or Cambridge.

After visiting the Duxford complex, I now hope we'll have a chance to explore the other IWM properties around Great Britain in the months to come.

London's Science Museum

When you think of London, you probably think
of traditionally famous sites like Buckingham Palace,
Westminster Abbey, Parliament, and the Tower of
London. But beyond those quintessentially London-
esque spots lie a lot of other amazing places to visit. It
is one of the world's largest cities, after all, so there is
life beyond the royals and Big Ben.

Scour any London Top 10 list, and you might see the
Science Museum listed. Here you're likely to find
more large groups of British school children than
large groups of tour buses. In fact, we were a little
overwhelmed by the crowds of kids. Fortunately,
there is so much geared toward energetic visitors,
young and old alike. Best of all, it's free to visit.

We started our time there by stopping by
the Information Desk to ask which exhibits our
children might find most interesting. We were
steered toward The Garden, the Pattern Pod, and the
Launchpad. My children loved them all, although I
think our favorite was the Pattern Pod, if for no other
reason than it was less crowded.

But the other areas of the museum that I passed
through seemed equally as interesting to children and
their parents. The museum covers everything from
space exploration to electronics to the human body. If
you've ever visited the Museum of Science and
Industry in Chicago, you'll find this to be a similar
experience.

A few tips if you plan a visit:

- Get there right when it opens at 10 a.m. This museum gets very crowded, very quickly. Enjoy as much time as you can before it really begins to fill up.

- Try to avoid school holidays and popular field trip time periods. We visited during my son's half term break in October. It was also the day before many other schools let out for the half-term, so there was a large number of field trips that day. I would have enjoyed our visit much more had it been less crowded.

- Dress coolly. If you take the Tube there (**South Kensington station**), you will only walk a few steps outdoors. The museum gets quite warm inside, so there's no need to bundle up.

- Visiting with young kids?
Check your pushchair in the cloakroom in the basement. We wasted a lot of our time there waiting on a lift to get from floor to floor. I wish instead we hadn't bothered with our stroller and could have taken the stairs. Also, buy the Science Museum's sticker book. You probably won't have time to look at it with your kids during the museum visit, but it will make a great activity book afterward, back in the hotel or on the flight home. My 4-year-old really enjoyed it and it's a fun and practical souvenir.

- Plan to eat lunch at the museum. There's a cafe or restaurant on almost every floor. This is such a huge building that you won't want to waste time leaving and re-entering just for a quick meal.

- Have particular interests? The staff at the information desk was really useful in helping us plan our time there. You'll also find a staff member stationed at each exhibit who can answer questions.

- Or just return the next day to see more. That's the best part of the free admission!

I'd love to get back again soon, as we barely covered a third of the museum.

If you've got a rainy day ahead of you (And let's face it, given that it's London, you probably will have at least one during an average trip!), the Science Museum is a great spot to put on your agenda.

Visiting Shakespeare Country

It was William Shakespeare who wrote "parting is such sweet sorrow," and that's exactly how I felt when it was time to leave Stratford-upon-Avon, his birthplace and final resting spot, after a fun day spent there. And while the picturesque English town, located between London and Birmingham in Warwickshire, is full of literary history, it also has something for travelers with all sorts of interests.

My first surprise was all the shopping. Naturally, there are plenty of souvenir shops, containing everything from baby bibs with Shakespeare quotes to Union Jack umbrellas. But you'll also find several large department stores and plenty of small, independent shops as well. Focus your time around Bards Walk and Henley Street, but you'll find plenty of shops scattered all over the town.

Even if you're not into history, the town itself is incredibly charming. We really enjoyed a long walk along the River Avon, which had wide paths, small dinghies bobbing around in the water, and lots of benches to admire the view. You'll also find street after street of Tudor homes. You'll want your camera at the ready, because each time I looked one way, I was more impressed than I was with my previous view.

Theatre performances abound, even those aimed at children. Book in advance to catch a show, but also know that you may stumble upon impromptu sonnets and famous Shakespeare verses by actors at the various Shakespeare sites around town.

Naturally, for history lovers you can't beat Stratford-upon-Avon. The life of Shakespeare dominates, but I think what I took away from my time here was more than just facts about this literary genius. I now have a much better understanding about what daily living was like during his lifetime.

So even if you don't know your Hamlets from your Macbeths, it's well worth a visit.

A few tips as you plan a trip:

- You can park in the town center (parking is plentiful, unlike in most historic British towns) and then walk to most of the attractions.

- If it's raining, I'd encourage you to buy a ticket on the bus tour that runs around town, so that you can maximize your sightseeing but avoid getting drenched.

- Think about anything that you've always wondered about Shakespeare, or favorite lines or scenes from his plays. You'll have many opportunities to ask questions of Shakespearean scholars and actors while you visit his home and other properties in town. I wish I had taken better advantage of these moments.

- Consider staying overnight. I know it's a popular place to go as a daytrip from London. But it is really difficult to see all the sites in one day, especially if you want to take time to shop or see a performance.

- The town and the Shakespeare attractions are surprisingly family-friendly, even for those with young kids..

I wondered out loud to my family if as a society we are a bit less smart than we were in Shakespeare's time, given our difficulty in understanding his work, at least upon first read. But I certainly feel smarter for having visited Stratford-upon-Avon and more knowledgeable about the life and times of this gifted writer.

Day Out in Windsor

I'm normally a pretty serious travel planner. I like to read as much as I can about a destination in anticipation of making the most of a visit somewhere, and so that I know more about what I'm seeing once I get there. But I also try to embrace spontaneity when I can, and so a very spur-of-the-moment trip to Windsor was an opportunity to enjoy a travel experience "in the moment" instead of "ahead of the moment."

Fortunately, visiting Windsor is particularly easy on an unprepared traveler. We quickly found a place to park. (Expect to pay approximately £10 for a 4-hour period in one of the central car parks.) Windsor is also easily accessible by train from London's Waterloo or Paddington stations, and the Windsor station is right in the center of town.

Our first stop was the obvious: Windsor Castle. Like a lot of Americans, I'm fairly fascinated by the royal family but wasn't all that well-versed on this castle. I wasn't entirely sure how often it was used or for what purpose, so I was excited to learn more. We were greeted at the entrance by perhaps the friendliest staff I've encountered at a tourist attraction in the UK. They assisted us in navigating the ticket booth (entrance fees are about £20 per adult) and security entrance process with our stroller and kids. And they were quick to point out that there was a family activity starting in about an hour, which was enormously helpful.

Upon entering the facility, you can pick up a free audioguide (they also have a children's version). This was really great to orient us to what we were seeing and gave us a deeper appreciation for the history of the castle and its various rooms. I highly recommend you pick one up, although I also tried to put it away at times so as to really take in my surroundings.

We spent some time exploring the outer walls of the castle and admired St. George's Chapel. Because we were visiting on a Sunday we weren't able to step inside, but it's stunning even from the exterior.

Then we entered the State Apartments, first admiring Queen Mary's Dolls' House exhibit. (I would have liked to spend more time examining these miniatures, but my interest was greater than that of my little boys.) Again, the audioguide will help to explain each of the rooms inside the castle. Because we were visiting in the winter, we also got to see the Semi-State Rooms. My favorite were the dining rooms. It was easy to imagine myself sitting down at one of those many, many chairs and feasting with all the notable people surrounding me. And don't miss the views out the windows. Unfortunately, you can't take photos inside the Castle, but I actually enjoyed the reprieve both in taking photos myself and in patiently waiting for others to do so.

After that, we headed to the family activity in the Moat Room, where our kids could color or create a paper castle. The whole family enjoyed the chance to step inside and rest a bit, while our children got to have some fun and activities geared more toward them.

You could also try to time your visit around the Changing of the Guard, which is usually around 11 a.m. except on Sundays. But even if you miss it, you'll see plenty of guards marching around. This was a real highlight for my little boys.

After leaving the castle, we headed out in search of lunch. You'll have plenty of choices, from family-friendly chain restaurants to independent pubs and cafes. The Windsor Royal Shopping complex would be a great place to head if the weather is unpleasant, as its indoor/outdoor concept would let you escape the elements. Fortunately, we visited on a beautiful day.

After lunch, we decided to cross the Thames and explore Eton a bit. The campus of the famous boys' school was closed to visitors that day, but we were still able to appreciate the quaintness of it, full of bookstores, antique shops and cafes. Well worth seeing if you're visiting Windsor anyway.

All in all, it was a wonderful day to take in such a culturally-significant spot. Because Buckingham Palace is only open to visitors in August and September, Windsor is a better bet if you want to peek inside a royal residence.

Exploring the White Cliffs of Dover

Many readers are probably familiar with Dover, either for the famous White Cliffs of Dover, or because it's an important port where ferries and cargo ships cross the English Channel. When planning a recent drive to Belgium via the Eurotunnel (which departs in nearby Folkestone), I wanted to allocate a night to explore this area and its deep history further. Many thanks to Visit Kent, the region's tourist organization, for helping me plan our trip.

DOVER CASTLE

Our first stop was Dover Castle. The sun was shining, a festival was on to entertain my young children, and it was clear that the day ahead was going to be full of fun for all of us. As you approach the castle, you'll immediately recognize why it was such an important piece of British history. It sits atop the cliffs, overlooking the water between England and France.

My children loved the details that make castles so magical for kids: drawbridges, catapults, towers, etc. And while my husband and I have grown accustomed to visiting castles as we've traveled throughout Europe, Dover sticks out for its wide ranging history. Its first beginnings as a Norman castle date back as early at 1066.

Its current form began to take shape in the 1160s by Henry II, but what I found most intriguing is that it was then updated and fortified following every war involving Britain between then and 1945. Needless to say, its importance in British military history is almost unmatched.

After exploring the castle itself and the grounds, we indulged our children in spending the rest of the day enjoying the entertainers at the festival being held that weekend. The castle does a wonderful job of hosting lots of varied events for the whole family throughout the year, so consider planning a visit around that schedule if you've got kids.

On a return visit, I'd love to explore the Secret Wartime Tunnels. For the first time, this underground shelter, which was used as far back as the Napoleon era right through to the Cold War, are open to the public to visit.

ACCOMMODATION: WALLETT'S COURT

After such an adventurous day out, we were quite pleased to kick up our feet in the beautiful Kent countryside at Wallett's Court. We were welcomed to the property so warmly, shown around, and then left to relax in our room. The family room at this hotel and spa was ideal for our family. A spacious room with enough beds for the four of us (difficult to find in Europe, particularly at smaller, independent properties), with a sliding door out to a beautiful patio and an enormous green garden.

Wallett's Court would make an equally appealing place to stay for a romantic night away, as the spa and the award-winning restaurant would allow you to spoil yourself in luxury without even getting in the car.

For the more adventurous, this property even offers glamping. You could spend the evening in a tipi or hut listening to the sounds of nature, and then awake to the birds chirping and the smells of your breakfast being cooked for you.

I think what I'll take away most from our night away in Dover at Wallett's Court was the serenity. It was so quiet, yet I felt comfortable allowing my children to make use of the gorgeous grounds. They ran around in the sunshine, challenging each other to races, while I sipped a Pimm's on the patio.

The next morning, instead of listening to them fight over what type of cereal to have, we all enjoyed a home-cooked breakfast in the hotel's conservatory. In short, we arrived at Wallett's tired and road-weary from our previous travels, and we left so refreshed. I wanted to bottle it up just like my cocktail from the previous afternoon.

WHITE CLIFFS OF DOVER

The next morning, before finishing our journey back to the East Midlands, we couldn't leave Dover without experiencing its most famous attraction: the White Cliffs. I saw the cliffs for the first time about a dozen years ago on a ferry from England to France. But this did little to prepare me for witnessing them up close (or as close as you can manage with two little boys hiking alongside you!).

There are lots of trails and footpaths that traverse the National Trust-owned property, allowing you to take in the views of the water and the cliffs at your own speed and ability. I could have stayed for a full morning and hiked for miles, it was that stunningly beautiful.

My boys were fascinated by the big boats you'll see coming into port. It's a nice mix of the modern purpose of this area, the natural beauty of it, and the history. You can't look out at that water, the French coast glimmering in the distance, and not be reminded of all that has transpired in the space between over thousands of years.

I definitely hope to return to Kent again soon. There's still much more to see, including Leeds Castle, Churchill's home, and Canterbury. But my stay in Dover was a great introduction to this beautiful and significant area of England.

My First Battle Proms Concert: The Concert with Spitfires

A couple of weeks ago, I attended my first Battle Proms event. If you're an American like me, you probably see the word prom and think only of the annual high school dance. But here in the UK, "Proms" is often referring to a famous series of classical music concerts held at the Prince Albert Hall in London each summer. Last summer, I vaguely recall seeing "Proms" on the television guide, airing on the BBC. I remember wondering what exactly "proms" might mean here, but in the midst of everything else I was learning about a new culture following our move a few weeks earlier, I didn't give it much more thought.

So needless to say, when my family was invited to join a few friends at a Battle Proms concert, I was excited to see what this "proms" stuff was all about!

Battle Proms is a little different from the actual Proms concerts in London, but a similar concept. I live very near Burghley House, which is considered to be England's greatest Elizabethan home and a popular tourist attraction. For the past several years, it's been host to one of several Battle Proms events held around the UK. I found this to be one of the most unique things my family has experienced since moving here, and I wanted to share a bit of the evening with you readers.

The evening began with couples, families and friends gathering on picnic blankets and lawn chairs throughout the sprawling gardens of the estate property. A large stage was set up, along with food and drink vendors, games for children, etc. We nibbled on treats, like pork pies, cheese and crackers, and crisps. The evening's entertainment began with a historic cavalry display. My little boys loved seeing the soldiers all dressed up and the various exercises they had their horses do. We were then treated to an amazing flyover by a Spitfire, the famous airplane used by the British Royal Air Force during World War II. It was incredibly moving as the plane swooped and twirled in the air above us for quite a while.

Then the true "proms" part of the evening began. The New England Symphony played many famous classical pieces, like the *1812 Overture* and *Beethoven's Battle Symphony*. One of the most memorable aspects was the cannons that were fired off during key points in these classical pieces (as many believe the composers intended for them to be played).

And the last 30 minutes or so of the concert were such a treat, especially to an American eager to learn more about British culture. The symphony played traditional British songs like *Jerusalem, Rule Britannia*, and *Land of Hope and Glory* (And *God Save the Queen*, naturally!), all while fireworks were being let off in the distance. The thousands of concert goers were all waving flags and singing along. It was definitely a moment I'll never forget.

I'm looking forward to tuning into the Proms concerts this summer on the BBC (it begins Friday night), but it'll never top seeing a Battle Proms performance in person. If you're planning a trip to Great Britain this summer, there are still several scheduled. Or plan ahead for next summer and include this special, classically British event in your itinerary.

My First Afternoon Tea

I'm a bit embarrassed to admit this (although I'm sure I've made far sillier confessions in this Dispatches column over the past year), but it took 16 months of living in Great Britain before I finally attended my first afternoon tea. I'm a busy mom, as are most of my friends here, so the opportunity to spend a couple of hours on a weekend afternoon relaxing over tea just doesn't present itself very often. But when my mother-in-law came for a visit with her sisters, it was the perfect moment for all of us to get introduced to this British cultural institution.

This being our first (and for them, perhaps only) afternoon tea experience, we selected the nicest hotel in the town where I live to go for tea. Unfortunately, the hotel did not take reservations (called a booking here), and even though we arrived promptly at 3:30 when the tea service began, the indoor dining areas were already full. Fortunately, there was space for us on the patio, and 5 minutes after we were seated, the sun began to shine.

We spent the first few minutes reading the menu. I think my favorite part of afternoon tea was that it involved lots of delicious food, not just the hot beverage. And in case you're not a tea drinker, no worries. They offered plenty of coffee and hot chocolate options too.

We selected the full champagne afternoon tea experience. We were first brought a glass of champagne. Then came a three-tiered tray of food, and pots of tea for each of us.

The bottom tier was different kinds of finger sandwiches (egg salad, roast beef, salmon, and cucumber and cream cheese). The middle tier was a variety of cakes. And the top tier was scones, clotted cream and homemade strawberry jam.

Having never attended an afternoon tea service before, we didn't know if there was a particular order in which we should eat the food. But we started with the savory sandwiches, then moved on to the scones, and finally the cakes. I felt absolutely stuffed by the time we finished, but it was so delicious.

If you're curious, all of this cost £27 pounds per person (about $43). Not exactly cheap, but considering I was so full I never ate dinner, I don't think it was outrageously priced. And no, if you're wondering, I have no idea how many calories I consumed that afternoon. Ignorance is bliss!

My only disappointment was the tea itself. I had expectations that we'd be served tea in beautiful, ornate tea pots and cups. Instead, it was served in the same basic white ceramic pots and cups that I get in any coffee shop around town.

Regardless, it was a wonderful and memorable experience. While it may have been my first afternoon tea, I'm fairly certain it won't be my last.

The Pure Joy of Hiking on Britain's Footpaths

One of my favorite discoveries since moving to Great Britain has been all the footpaths and bridleways around the country. I've always enjoyed hiking, but in the US, this has typically been confined to trails at local, state or national parks. Whereas here it seems that nearly all villages are connected via a series of paths through the countryside that are accessible to the public. They often run through or adjacent to private land, but anyone is allowed to use them.

When I first began hiking these trails, friends back in the US asked me how I knew of these paths or where to go. The first way was just to pay attention to the signs for them. They're typically marked by green signs that say footpath or bridleway. Sometimes the sign will designate where the path leads, other times not.

Other times I learn of nice walks to take by reading about them in local magazines or newsletters. Rambling, as it is often called here, is a popular hobby, particularly with dog walkers. So these local publications often introduce routes to their readers. I especially like these recommendations because they are often circular instead of one-way, saving me from having to retrace my steps. They also give the approximate length of time and level of difficulty.

But the best way to plan a route is to use the ordnance survey tool. My local library carries the paper maps, but in the digital age, the web is probably your best bet.

One of the reasons I often don't do much planning of my walks in advance is that I enjoy the serendipity of making surprise discoveries along the way. I've learned of abandoned manor homes, gorgeous hidden churches, small ponds, even an old Roman road dating back to AD 61. Indeed, many of these trails have quite a long history, as they're often based on old roads and horse paths.

My only negative experience on a footpath was when I followed one that led me straight to a sewage treatment plant. Yuck.

I recently learned the difference between a footpath and bridleway. A footpath is intended to be just for walkers, while a bridleway can be used for horseback riding and bicycling.

You can certainly plan entire holidays and trips around hiking and utilizing these trails. I was just in the Lake District a few weeks ago and it was clear that most of the fellow tourists were there for that reason (as was my own family). But I think what I like best about this form of recreation is that these paths are found everywhere. I don't think I've been to a village yet that didn't have at least one footpath leading in and out of it.

Great Travel Planning Resources for Your Next Trip to GB

I got a lot of great feedback from my post last week about things to know about British holidays (*thanks*!). Several of you mentioned it was helpful, and I know many of you are always planning your next trip to Great Britain (not matter how far into the future that may be). I thought it made sense to continue on the topic of travels around the country, and share a few of my favorite travel planning resources.

All-Around Resources:

Anglotopia.net: Duh! If you're reading this you probably already know what a fabulous job Jonathan and his wife do pulling together information from many different sources, as well as their own profound knowledge of all things GB. I particularly love the details they share about the history of various attractions around the country. Since I'm always traveling with young children, I don't often get to linger reading signage or spending hours in quiet museums. I rely on this site for a lot of that background info (either before or after I visit a place).

National Trust and English Heritage: If you travel to experience the history of this country, these are unbeatable websites. I love being able to pop in the postcode of where we're staying (or our house!) and see what's closest to us and get all the details about visiting.

TripAdvisor.co.uk: This site is not without its flaws. I never use it as my exclusive travel planning resource because I find it can often be clouded by a few readers' misguided reviews. However, I rarely visit an attraction or restaurant (especially if it's pricey) without first reading reviews on this site. I can usually get a sense of what to look out for, what I should consider avoiding, and what's just not worth my precious travel dollars.

Train Travel:

Seeing Great Britain by train often makes the most sense, especially for Americans who may be a bit daunted by driving on the opposite side of the road. But train travel can feel almost as foreign if you're not used to traveling this way. These resources will help guide you through the process.

National Rail Enquiries: Definitely the most comprehensive site for planning your rail journeys. Their stations and destinations page allow you to figure out how to get to popular attractions around the country via train.

The Man in Seat 61: I first stumbled upon this site when booking tickets on the Eurostar train to Paris. I was a little overwhelmed by which carriage to choose when booking our seats, and realized this website breaks down the various options really well. Turns out, the site covers rail travel all over the world, and the UK in great depth. It's a handy resource, especially if you're picky about your seat.

Raileasy: Someone tipped me off to this site because, as they explained, sometimes traveling from one destination to another is cheaper if you "split the fare." Meaning instead of paying the regular price of the ticket from Point A to Point B, you actually buy separate tickets for all the stops along the way from A to B. It doesn't really make sense to me, but sometimes it comes out a bit cheaper. Regardless, it's worth checking this site before you buy especially for a long, expensive journey.

Traveling with Children:

If you're planning a trip to Great Britain and you're bringing the kids along, you can't go wrong with these resources at your fingertips.

Britain with Kids Guidebook: I checked this book out from our local library not long after we moved here, and I loved it so much I bought my own copy. It's now full of post-it notes, scribbles and highlights and I'm guessing I'll wear it out completely by the time we move back to the US. Its recommendations, from fun days out with children, to lodging, to restaurants, are invaluable. We have yet to disagree with any of its suggestions.

Day Out with the Kids: I find this site tends to be my go-to place whenever we have a rainy day, whether we're home or traveling around the UK. You simply plug in your postcode, and up pops up tons of ideas within a certain number of miles from where you are. But of course, you can use it for sunny days, too!

Special Events:

Red Letter Days: I was booking tickets to the Battle Proms concert in our town when I found this website. They were offering tickets to the event for quite a bit cheaper than the host site. I quickly learned it was a great site, not just for saving money, but for getting ideas for other outings. If you're looking to do something really unique or want to plan a once-in-a-lifetime activity on your next trip, it's a great place to find inspiration.

The Festival Calendar: I have no scientific data to back up my opinion on this, but I'm convinced there are more festivals and big events taking place here per square mile than in the US. I feel like there's something big happening every weekend, especially in the spring and summer months. This site does a pretty good job of keeping track of it all. If you love festivals and concerts, it's definitely one to bookmark.

Happy travel planning, everyone!

Key Differences Between the UK and Continental Europe

Anyone with a map could tell you that there's a divide between the UK and the rest of continental Europe, but there's more than just the English Channel that divides the two geographic bodies. There are cultural differences as well, some serious, some trivial. I've spent the last two years living in England, and have traveled around Europe fairly extensively. I thought I'd share a few differences, especially from a visitor's perspective.

Driving

You'll find narrow lanes and twisty curves whether you're in York or Germany, but you'll only find yourself driving on the left side of the road in the UK and Ireland, not continental Europe.

Money

The UK is in the European Union, so you may have assumed that meant the euro was the form of currency used here. But the UK still uses the pound sterling. There's a lot of history to that decision, which I won't go into (mostly because it's not something I know a lot about). The only other time we haven't used the euro during our travels was in Denmark, Sweden and Norway.

Denmark has the same opt-out clause that the UK has, Sweden hasn't yet joined the European Exchange Rate Mechanism which is a condition of adopting the euro, and Norway isn't in the European Union.

There are several other countries that haven't yet met the requirements to adopt the euro.

From a practical point of view, the euro is very convenient. Whenever we return home from a trip in Europe, we never exchange whatever cash we have remaining. We just save it for the next trip over, since most of the countries we have plans to visit use the euro. And it's a currency we've become familiar with, just like the pound, so we don't have to re-learn what various coins look like each time we visit Europe.

What always strikes me as funny is that there are some coin machines here that will take either a pound or a euro coin (like grocery trolleys). If I have any leftover euro coins from trips, I always stash them in my car to use for that purpose.

Electrical Voltage

Travels to continental Europe include yet another voltage change. Most European countries use a 220-volt system, but the UK uses 240. However, there has been an effort to harmonize this. Many products are now rated 230, which means they could be used with either voltage. The issue then becomes the outlet style itself. You'll need an adapter to plug in a British electrical device in Europe (and vice versa) because the three-prong style is used in the UK and the two-prong style is used in Europe.

Food

Obviously there are tons of variations in diet across borders around the world. Anyone who has traveled abroad knows this. It's one of the things that makes travel interesting (and delicious).

There are two things always jump out at me when comparing Great Britain and Europe though (one serious and one trivial). The trivial? Sandwich style. In Europe, freshly baked baguettes are the norm, with a variety of fillings like cured meats and soft cheeses, as a quick snack or light lunch. In Great Britain, it's what I call the "triangle sandwich": standard slices of bread, cut diagonally and pre-packaged with fillings like egg and cress, tuna and sweet corn, and roast chicken. (Yes, you can get baguettes here, but it's not the go-to sandwich the way it is in many European countries.) Either way, it's healthier than a burger in fries, right?

The more serious issue? Obesity. The UK is the most obese country in the European Union and in my opinion, it's quite obvious as you travel around, both here and in Europe. I'm not quite sure why this is. Maybe it's diet (fish and chips aren't exactly low calorie) or lifestyle, or a combination of both. Of course, the problem is far worse in the US.

Observations from Wales

Last weekend, for the first May bank holiday weekend, we spent three days exploring the beautiful Snowdonia region of Wales. This was our first time visiting another country in the UK other than England while we've been living here, and I was excited to experience what made Wales different (but more importantly, what made Wales wonderful!).

I am by no means an expert on anything Welsh. After all, I only spent three days there, and only in one particular region, but I still thought it would be interesting to share some observations about what I loved and what made me want to see more of this gorgeous country. For those who have been or who live there, I'd love to hear your thoughts in the comments of this post.

The Ruralness

My family has traveled to some remote areas. Our trip to Ireland last summer took us to a very area. The cottage we rented in Snowdonia was by far the most remote place we've stayed. Sheep and hills stretched for miles all around us, and it was a 20-minute drive to the closest store, and it was the size of what most we would call a convenience store.

Obviously not all of Wales is this rural. Cardiff, for example, is a city of almost 350,000 people. But Snowdonia's population is approximately 25,000 people and is 2,100 sq. kilometers in size. (Rhode Island is 3,140 sq. km with a population of over 1 million people, for comparison.)

The Beauty

I was simply blown away by how gorgeous it was there. One of the most scenic hikes I've ever taken was at the base of Mt. Snowdon, the tallest peak. Needless to say, with two small children, we didn't attempt to reach the summit, but just staring up at the mountains all around us was thrilling enough for us. We also hiked down to waterfalls, through rolling green sheep pastures, and around beautiful lakes. If you love this type of activity, Wales is definitely the place to be.

Welsh Language

I knew just from researching our trip in advance and finding the spellings of certain locations to be quite difficult to spell, that the Welsh language was very different from English or any romance-based language. It was so fun to challenge my 6-year-old, who just learned to read last year, to try to pronounce some things when he saw signs all around us. I enjoyed listening to it spoken, also. As someone who is very interested in foreign languages, I loved that it added another cultural dimension to our trip there. I heard it spoken quite often during our weekend, so I was surprised to read online later that according to the 2011 UK census, 73% of residents of Wales report having no Welsh language skills.

Castles

I've lost track of how many castles we have visited throughout our European travels these past two years. Lucky us! We really enjoy the history that comes alive when you go to one, the beauty of the structures, and the fact that our kids enjoy walking around them is a bonus.

Wales has so many wonderfully preserved castles to offer visitors. We toured Conwy Castle and it's probably been my favorite of any. It has everything you'd want from a castle, like breathtaking views from towers, a suspension bridge, a moat, and the walls that surround the old town limits. It is considered one of the best surviving medieval castles.

My only disappointment of the trip was that I never got to try a Welsh rarebit. (This, to my understanding, is sort of like an open-faced grilled cheese sandwich, only much better!) It's been on my list of British foods I want to eat while living here, and I figured that was the place, but it wasn't on the menu at any of the restaurants we visited. So I guess I just have to make a return trip.

We're heading to Scotland later this month, and I plan to write a similar post about observations from that country, too. And I've love to get to Northern Ireland soon too, to complete the United Kingdom "Grand Tour."

Observations from Scotland

A few weeks ago, I shared some observations that I made while on a brief trip to Wales from where we live in England. For the second May bank holiday weekend, we ventured up to Scotland, and so I thought I'd share a few observations about differences I noted while there. (Again, I am by no means an expert on life in Scotland; these are just a few things I thought were interesting after spending a few days there.)

The Scottish Accent

Unlike in Wales, we didn't hear any locals speaking any language other than English. But it almost seemed like we were. The Scottish accent is one of my favorites, and I thought I was ready for it. Our neighbors are Scottish, and I can understand them just fine. But when you hear two Scottish people talking to each other, that's a whole different story! It's so thick and different from both the American and English accent that I had trouble making out what some people were saying. It's still absolutely lovely to listen to, though!

Friendly, Outgoing People

Before we moved here, people warned us that the English weren't that friendly. I actually don't find that to be true at all, but I will say that English people in general are a bit more reserved than Americans. They tend to be less forward with personal questions. However, in Scotland, we found the people to be extremely friendly and outgoing.

They asked us lots of questions and happily answered our questions. (I should note, there's no right or wrong way to be friendly. I appreciate the English reserve just as much sometimes. It can be refreshing not to discuss personal matters with complete strangers, after all.)

Lots of Cattle

The first thing I noticed when we crossed the border into Scotland was that there were tons of cows grazing in the fields. Still plenty of sheep too, of course, just like in England and Wales, but I saw so many cows too! It then occurred to me that most of the beef I buy in the supermarket is labeled as being from Scotland. And sure enough, a quick Google search revealed that the beef industry is the largest sector of the Scottish economy.

Discovered by Global Tourists

Another thing that surprised me was how we were surrounded by tourists from around the world everywhere we went. To be fair, we were in tourist areas, like Edinburgh, Stirling and Loch Lomond. But I have to say, outside of London and popular day trips from London, I rarely run into tourists from elsewhere in the world when we travel around England. It's mostly just other British people on a day out or on a holiday when we are visiting castles and such elsewhere in England. Scotland reminded me of Ireland in this way. Even when we were out in the country, it was common to see tour buses full of tourists rambling by.

Different Paper Money

Now don't go running to exchange your pounds when leaving England for Scotland. Scotland definitely uses the pound as their currency. But when we paid cash for things and were given change, the paper bills looked slightly different from our typical £5 and £10 bills. It had some Scottish "flair."

Unfortunately, we didn't have any left at the end of the trip, because I was curious to spend them here in England and see if it was a hassle to use them. I suspect it wouldn't be. I'd love to know more about the history of this. Perhaps someone can explain it to me in the comments!

Anyone interested in British politics knows that Scotland has dominated the headlines in the past two years while I've been living here. It was really fun to be able to cross the border and experience life in Scotland, even if it was for just a few days. I hope I get a chance to return before our time on "the island" is over.

Camping Comparisons Between England and the US

One of my family's hobbies is to go camping. We try to plan at least one weekend trip per summer, and I think we've managed to do it each of the years I've been married (so almost 12 years now!). Both my husband and I camped when we were kids, and it's fun to introduce this way of traveling to our own children.

So naturally, when we moved to England we thought it would be fun to experience camping here as well. Here are a few observations from our camping weekends in England:*

Campfires

In the US, you'd hardly bother to camp without a campfire. I know occasionally that's limited if there are concerns about forest fires, but for the most part, I've never camped where you couldn't have a fire in America. We've always cooked most of our meals over the campfire, and then enjoyed the fire for well into the night. (Plus, you can't have s'mores without one!) In England it's not as prevalent, and most campgrounds we've found don't allow it. We were shocked our first camping trip to learn we couldn't have one. And the reason we chose the particular campground where we stayed this weekend in Somerset was specifically because they DO allow campfires. (Thank you, Petruth Paddocks!)

Setting

In the US, I've mostly camped at state or national park campgrounds, and an occasional privately-run campground. Most of these have been in the woods, so each campsite is surrounded by trees.

In England, I've only stayed in privately-run campgrounds, and they've all been a giant, open field (or a series of fields, depending on how large of an operation it is). I have to say that I miss the privacy these wooded sites provide, although my kids enjoy running around the fields and playing football (soccer).

Campsites

In the US, I've always reserved a campsite in advance, and have been assigned (or chosen) the exact campsite. Here in England, I've booked a spot in advance, but I haven't known exactly where we'll pitch our tent until we arrive on-site and we're directed where to go. Most of the fields haven't even had clearly defined or numbered sites, staff just points to a general area in the field where you should go.

Tents, RVs, etc.

One of the things I enjoy doing while camping is walking around the campground and seeing the setups of other campers. You usually see a mix of tents (large and small), RVs (again, large and small), pop-up campers, etc. Some have electrical hookups, some don't. Most have their camp chairs and portable tables set up, too, as well as supplies for cooking and coolers. This is all relatively similar in both the US and England from my experience.

Fire Pits and Picnic Tables

I've never camped at a campground in the US that didn't provide some type of fire pit and at least one picnic table for each campsite. Conversely, I've never camped in England where either of those were provided (in keeping with the lack of campfires, of course)!

I really miss the extra surface space and dining space that a picnic table provides, especially when I'm trying to prepare a meal for my family. We end up eating picnic-style on blankets on the ground (or from our laps while seated in camping chairs). This weekend, the campground provided temporary fire pits to each site that wanted to have a campfire.

It's probably clear from my post that overall, I miss the style of camping I had come to expect from the places I've been in the US. I have definitely enjoyed camping in England, but it is different.

*I specifically say England here because we haven't had the opportunity to camp in Scotland, Wales or Northern Ireland, and I can't speak to how that might be different.

An American Tours Buckingham Palace

A perfect example of how naïve I was when I first moved to England 2 ½ years ago occurred when my family visited Buckingham Palace on our first day trip into London. I hadn't actually planned to go inside, considering we had two young children with us. But I never realized that typically, a tourist can't go inside anyway. After all, this is the Queen's home and is actively used almost year-round.

When a friend of mine organized a day trip into the city to tour the Palace during one of the few weeks it is open to visitors each year, I jumped at the chance to step inside and see it with my own eyes.

As this is such an iconic place for Britain, I thought I'd share a few thoughts about the experience.

- Each year when it opens, there's always a special exhibition of some kind. In the past, it's been anything from some of the Queen's diamond collection, to Kate Middleton's wedding dress. This year, it was a collection of some of the most iconic photos ever taken of the Queen, in celebration of her achieving the milestone of Britain's longest reigning monarch. The photos were stunning and it felt like such an amazing time to be able to see her Palace, within a few weeks of that momentous occasion.

- The tour for our group was actually a three-stage process. We had purchased tickets as part of the "Royal Day Out" package, which meant we had admission to the Royal Mews (the stables and garages), the State Rooms (the Palace itself) and the Queen's Gallery (an art gallery with a frequently changing exhibition). We were welcome to visit the Royal Mews and the State Rooms whenever we wanted, but we had a timed ticket to the gallery (mostly as a means of crowd control since it is a relatively small space).

- Naturally, the State Rooms were a real highlight. I've visited a few other royal attractions, most notably Windsor Castle, and yet Buckingham Palace has an amazingly spectacular feel to it. The dining room in particular blew me away and I loved learning about all the effort that goes into preparing for official functions like a state visit. Another highlight was having the "secret entrance" that the family uses to go in and out of their private residence into the more public spaces.

- The Royal Mews surprised me. I almost suggested our group skip it because we were really pressed for time. But I absolutely loved it. The carriages are truly spectacular when you're able to get so close to them. And I think because the Queen is such an avid equestrian and horse lover, this area has taken on a real importance under her reign.

- At all three venues you're provided with a free audioguide, which really helps you to better understand and appreciate what you're seeing. It can be a bit distracting to see everyone wandering around with the guides glued to their ears but I was grateful for these devices as it really enhanced my visit.

- There were a few moments that were particularly special to an American. A gift given to the Duke of Edinburgh from President Obama (custom Fell Pony bits and shanks) was on display in the stables. A gift from President George W. Bush (a porcelain bowl and platter) was on display in the Palace as part of a small exhibit showing some of the gifts given to the Queen during state visits, and the dress the Queen wore for President Obama's state visit was on display as well.

- The thing that made the biggest impression on me after visiting might surprise you though. I was completely blown away by the acreage found outside the Palace itself. There are 38 acres of green space behind the Palace. In the center of London! I couldn't believe how quiet and peaceful it was back there. My friends and I decided that instead of crashing a state dinner, we'd much rather crash one of the famous garden parties held on the back lawn each summer. (Your Majesty, if you're reading, please feel free to put me on the guest list!)

A few other helpful hints if you'd like to see it for yourself:

- The State Rooms are typically only open in August and September. The 2016 open dates are not yet posted on the Royal Collection website.

- The Royal Mews are typically open from February-early November.

- The Queen's Gallery is open year-round, though not daily. It's a better destination for art lovers than royal enthusiasts, however. I enjoyed my time there, but more for the beautiful art, not as a way of learning more about the Royal family.

- If, like me, you're also fascinated with the outdoor space at the Palace, tours of the garden were available. I'd definitely try to catch one should I ever have a chance to visit again.

- Plan to buy some postcards or a coffee-table style book in one of the gift shops. You can't take photos in the State Rooms, so you'll want some way of remembering the amazing interior that you were lucky enough to see.

My Favorite British Travel Destinations

Our time living in England will come to an end in a few months, and I'm beginning to mentally process what that will mean for us emotionally.

The greatest experiences by far have been our travels, both within Great Britain's borders and elsewhere in Europe. In this post, I'll only highlight our favorite British travels given Anglotopia's focus.

In no particular order:

The Lake District

If I had to choose the most gorgeous scenery of our British travels, I think I'd give the award to the Lake District. Everywhere you looked seemed like a scene out of a movie. And all the villages we passed through were incredibly charming.

London

To be just a short train ride from London was one of the biggest appeals to us about moving to England. And while we didn't do as many day trips as we would have liked, I will count our days exploring the city as some of my very favorite. I'm excited for another Christmas Eve spent exploring the city later this month, and hopefully another day or two still to come for my family.

Wales

We planned our first long weekend in Wales last May, mostly to just "check it off the list" of places we wanted to see. But it's been unexpectedly one of our best trips to date. Snowdonia was so rural and so naturally wild that we just loved hiking the hills and taking it all in. We're visiting a different area of Wales next weekend and I'm truly looking forward to seeing more of this beautiful country.

Scotland

I really wish we had devoted more of our travel time to seeing Scotland. We only had a few days there, so we focused on Edinburgh and the southern part of the Highlands. By some stroke of luck, we had great weather while there, so it was extra special to get to see such a beautiful place with the sun shining on it.

Cornwall

I had never heard of Cornwall before we moved to England, but I'm so glad I had the chance to visit. It was quite a drive from where I live, but the coast was so ruggedly beautiful and the overall feeling in that part of England was that it has a culture all its own. I only wish I could have experienced it during the summer to better appreciate its beautiful beaches.

Norfolk

I'll always think of Brancaster in Norfolk as my family's own little seaside getaway. It was close enough to visit as a day trip, and watching my boys learn to love the beach as much as I do during our time there is a true highlight for me.

Cambridge

Only a 45-minute drive from our house, this was a favorite place to take visitors. Certainly seeing the beautiful buildings of the university is impressive, and punting is so much fun. But I was mostly taken by the history of the place, and its charming shops, twisty streets, and "academic" vibe.

York

The history in York rivals that of any European city I've been to, yet it's a completely manageable size to do in a weekend. The shopping and museums are incredible, also, so it's one of those places that has a little something for everyone.

There are still so many places I hope to see before we leave (Bath, Oxford, Devon, Isle of Skye, I could go on and on...), but I'm forever grateful for the memories of the places we have managed to get to.

Getting a UK Driving Licence

The First Steps and The Costs

I finally earned my UK driver's license last week. When an American moves to the UK, you have 12 months to obtain a UK driver's license if you plan to legally drive while here. (Time length and requirements vary depending on which country you move here from.) It was a complicated, time-consuming and expensive process from start to finish, so for my next series of posts, I'm going to share all that I learned from it.

Keep in mind, this is the process you undertake when you already have a valid international driver's license, meaning you are licensed to drive in another country (for me, the US). I'm not sure of the process when you're 17 and a true "learner" here, although I think it's roughly the same.

In this post, I'm going to outline the steps I took and the costs. I'll break down some of these steps in greater detail in upcoming posts, so if this is a topic that interests you, stay tuned. Bear in mind that you can't proceed to another step without first completing the prior step. In other words, I couldn't schedule my theory test until I had received my provisional license. So there's usually a wait of several weeks between some of these steps.

1. Obtain a provisional driver's license. This is done via forms filled out and submitted. Cost: £50 (With an added cost of £5 to get a picture taken to include on the license)

2. Purchase preparatory materials. (Not required, but it would be very difficult to pass

the theory test without studying this information in advance.) Cost: £13 on Amazon.co.uk

3. Take the driving theory test. This is an electronic test done in a test center, asking question regarding driving rules and laws, as well as hazard perception videos that test your reactions. Cost: £31

4. Participate in driving lessons. (Not required, but very typical to do in order to have a better chance at passing.) Cost varies. My instructor charged £30 per hour and I took 8 hours of lessons. I think this was on the high end.

5. Purchase "L" plates for my car for the driving practical test. Cost: £6 at Halfords

6. Take the driving practical test. 40 minutes out on the roads with an examiner. Cost: £63

Total cost for me to obtain my driver's license: £408 (approximately $683)

While I think my lessons were pricey, many people do not pass the theory test or the driving test the first time, meaning they are charged the £31 or £63 fees two or more times to take it again. I felt it better to invest in a lot of lessons up front, and therefore give myself the best chance of passing the practical test on the first try. (Which, I'm proud to say, I did!)

Getting a Provisional License

You may remember from last week's Dispatches from England column that I'm writing a series of posts on the process of obtaining a UK Driver's License and what I learned along the way. I outlined the steps and costs last week.

The first step was the easiest, which was obtaining a Provisional License. This is the UK equivalent to what we call a Learner's Permit in the US. Because I have a valid driver's license from another country, the restrictions that often apply to someone just learning to drive with a provisional license did not apply to me. In other words, I didn't have to have a licensed driver in the car with me at all times, I was allowed on the motorways, etc., but I did need the permit itself.

It was a fairly straight forward process. We just filled out a form online, which asked us the basic questions you'd expect: our addresses for the past three years (which was only one address for us, since they were only interested in UK addresses), birthdate, passport details, etc. We had to notify them if we wore eyeglasses or had any vision or health issues that would affect our driving.

And of course, we had to pay £50.

We faced a couple of different challenges to complete the process, however. First, we needed to provide them with a passport-style photo.

Because both my husband and I have had our passports for a few years, we no longer had an extra copy of our photo. So we had to use a photo booth kiosk at a local grocery store to take the appropriate type of photo for our provisional license (which later was transferred to my driver's license). That cost an additional £5 per person.

The final challenge was that we had to submit our US passports to the DVLA (the UK equivalent to the BMV or DMV in the US). It made us very nervous to drop our passports in the post, not knowing exactly when we'd get them back. Those are our only valid form of identification as expats, so understandably that was a little alarming to give up. It was also one of the big reasons we couldn't apply for our licenses right away. My husband travels internationally for work quite often, and we had to find a window of time when he could be without his passport for a few weeks. Fortunately, within 3 weeks we had them back in our possession. It was quite a relief to see those show up in our mail slot!

The important aspect of the provisional license process is that it establishes you as a driver in this country. We set up online accounts for ourselves via this process, which later allowed us to schedule our theory and practical driving tests. And if you get a speeding ticket while driving with a provisional license, it still counts against you. (Don't ask me how I know this!) :) The provisional license step was my favorite out of the whole process, though: no tests to study for!

British Words and Terms on the Driving Theory Test

I'm continuing this week with the process of obtaining a UK Driver's License. Next up is the Driving Theory Test. This is the computerized assessment of your knowledge of road rules and laws. I'll tell you all about the test itself in a future post, but the first step for me was studying!

In the process of studying for the theory test, my husband and I took a lot of practice tests and answered a lot of sample questions. We started keeping track of some of the words and terms that popped up that we had never heard before (despite having driven in the country for the previous six months!). Some of them made us chuckle, others made us scratch our heads.

- **Dipped headlights.** I was really confused by this term at first, because it's actually just your regular headlights. By adding the term "dipped" I thought it meant some other variation of headlights. High beams are called the same here.

- **Dazzle.** Speaking of headlights, this is the term for when you become blinded or disoriented by another driver's headlights. There were a lot of questions about how to avoid dazzling other drivers. Perhaps we use the same word in the US for this. I honestly don't know!

- **Toucan, pelican, puffin and zebra crossings.** You might think we were studying for a trip to the zoo when we memorized the various pedestrian, bicycle and tram crossing types that exist here, with their crazy animal names. I still don't understand how they got these names, but I have learned the differences between them. (I won't bore you with the differences. They mostly relate to whether there is a traffic light to accompany the crossing, and whether the crossing is only for pedestrians or also includes cyclists or trams.)

- **Traffic calming, contraflow, box junction, and chicane.** These are all measures or techniques used to control traffic patterns, reduce gridlock and in some cases, the speed of drivers. Not being from an urban area of the US, and I don't live in an urban area in the UK, I wasn't familiar with some of these methods firsthand in either country.

- **MOT certificate.** I had heard of this prior to studying for the test, mostly from commercials on the radio for auto body shops, but I wasn't sure what it was. Turns out that many vehicles are required to have a MOT test to determine its road safety and environmental standards. This is different than having your car serviced, though. An annual MOT test is required of any car over 3 years of age.

Taking Driving Lessons

I'm continuing on with the next step in my series on obtaining a UK driver's license. (And by the way, to answer those who have commented on this, yes, I know it is spelled licence here. I'll continue to use US spellings in my columns for the foreseeable future.)

After studying for and passing my driving theory test, it was then time to begin preparing for the actual driving test. While it is not mandatory, several people recommended that I take a driving lesson or two prior to taking the test. Given that I only had a couple of months until our 1-year deadline to get our license came around, I really wanted to increase my chances of passing the test the first time, so I signed up with an instructor who was recommended to us.

In hindsight, I spent way too much time on this, and far too much money. My instructor charged 30 pounds per hour, and I took 8 hours of lessons (a total of 240 pounds, which is equivalent to $400). Some instructors charge 20-25 pounds, and I really think I could have learned what I needed in just 3-4 hours of lessons. My husband took a 2-hour training prep class with an instructor and passed his test.

It is also a bit awkward. I've been driving for nearly 20 years, and so to have someone sitting next to me in the car critiquing what I was doing was really nerve-wracking. But it was still worthwhile. Here were just a few things that I learned to focus on, which helped to ensure I passed my test a few weeks later.

- **Mirror, signal, maneuver.** You'll hear lots of driving students reference MSM, which is short for mirror, signal, maneuver. It's the order you must use whenever you carry out a maneuver (like changing lanes or turning). One thing I realized during the course of my lessons is that I had fallen into a habit of signaling first, and then checking my mirrors before I moved. Obviously I had to switch this around.

- **Proper steering wheel control.** Like many drivers, I had also gotten into the habit of letting my steering wheel slide through my hands once I had completed a turn, or I sometimes grabbed it the wrong way when turning. So this was something I worked on and practiced during lessons. I didn't have too much trouble remembering to keep both hands on the steering wheel, but my instructor said many drivers struggle with this.

- **Specialty maneuvers.** In the course of your driving test, you'll be expected to carry out a particular maneuver. It could just be backing into a parking space. Or parallel parking. Or turning around in the road. The one I had to do on my test is called a left reverse. I basically had to back into a side street to my left. These are certainly all things I had done before while driving, but it was good to practice with a professional who taught me a few tricks to make the maneuvers smooth and to help me better control my car.

I'll be sharing more about my actual test in a future post.

Taking the UK Theory Driving Test

Last week, I challenged you to answer some sample questions from the UK Theory Driving Test. Pretty tough, right? So what's it like to actually take the full test (which is step 2 of the process of obtaining a UK Driver's License)?

First, you'll book the date and time online. I chose a Saturday morning, so off I went before the sun came up to one of the testing centers near our house (about 30 minutes away). The test center was actually inside a shopping mall. I was greeted by the receptionist, who asked to see my provisional license. I was then given instructions for putting all my belongings, especially my phone, in a locker, and then I waited for the other people taking their test to arrive.

Once we were all there, we were taken into a room with enough computers for each of us (there were about 10 of us being tested that morning). There was a glass wall where a test administrator observed us for the duration of the test. I sat down at one of the computers, put on the provided headset, and began the test.

The first part of the test was similar to the questions I shared last week. There were about 40-45 multiple choice questions, and then for the last few questions (50 in total), we had to read a few paragraphs about a driving scenario and then answer questions about what we would do if we were the driver. Out of these 50 questions, you had to get 43 correct in order to pass. I'm proud to say I only missed 1!

The next part of the test was (for me) the most difficult. I watched a series of 14 videos, which was basically a camera mounted to the dashboard of a car. In each video there would be 1-2 "incidents" that would force the driver to react. Anything from a pedestrian walking out in the street, to a giant puddle that needs to be avoided. You had to click the mouse when you first noticed the hazard. For each hazard, you receive a score of 1-5 depending on how quickly you reacted. (5 being the best.)

In theory, it sounds pretty simple, but my driving instructor informed me that for experienced drivers, it's actually a little tricky. It's possible to react too quickly, and not have your "click" counted by the system. He encouraged me to click a few times whenever I noticed something. But you have to be careful... if you click too much, you might get a score of zero for "over clicking."

If you're curious to know more, or see how you'd fare, you can take a practice test for free here.

It took me about 45 minutes (and cost me £31). I was very relieved to have my "You passed!" letter in hand, which then allowed me to schedule my actual driving test.

All About Finally Passing My UK Driving Test

I'm wrapping up my series of posts on the process and experience of obtaining a UK driver's license. The final step is obviously the driving test itself. I'll walk you through my test to give you a sense of what it was like.

I arrived to the test center about 15 minutes early and waited in the waiting room. While I waited, I watched three others hoping to get their license pull back into the parking lot and be told they had failed. (It was obvious by their reaction.) Needless to say, that made me a little nervous.

I was then greeted by one of the examiners who walked me to my car. She checked my paperwork. Then the test began when she asked me a couple of questions about my car. This is referred to as the "show me tell me" portion of the test, which is designed to show the examiner how well you know the workings of your car. I was asked to open the hood of the car, describe how I would check the oil level, and to point to the brake fluid. Luckily I was prepared for this, and knew just what to say and where to point.

Then we got in the car and the driving began. The examiner gave me clear instructions all along the way (so it's not necessary to know how to get from point A to point B on your own, which was helpful to me since the test center was about 30 minutes from my house in a town I rarely visit).

She occasionally made notes on her paper (which again made me a bit nervous), but mostly we either rode in silence or chatted. She usually only asked me questions when we were stopped at a red light or in traffic.

Beyond just driving around and having her observe me, there were several portions of the 45-minute test that were mandatory components.

1) Carry out a maneuver. I knew I'd be asked to either back into a parking space, parallel park, do a left reverse into a side street, do a right reverse into a side street, or do a turnaround in the road. I was hoping I'd get to do one of the parking ones as I felt the most comfortable with that. Naturally, instead I was asked to do a left reverse into a side street. I definitely didn't execute it perfectly, but did well enough to get by.

2) Drive on the motorway. I also knew I'd spend a portion of the test driving on the motorway. This was the part I was least nervous about, as I find driving on the motorway to be quite easy here. It's frankly not all that different from driving on a US highway.

3) Drive for 10 minutes without instructions. My driving instructor had also prepared me for this portion of the test. The examiner simply asked me to follow the signs for the "university" and for the next 10 minutes, I did that and drove toward the university without any directions or instructions from her. Apparently it is designed to ensure drivers are comfortable getting around without someone telling them where to go. Again, as an adult with years of experience driving, this wasn't difficult for me.

So how did I do? During the course of my test, I had 4 minor faults. You're allowed 15, so I felt quite good about this. Apparently there were two times when I started driving after being stopped (like at a red light) without first checking my mirror. And she gave me two faults for issues during my left reverse into the side street.

While you're allowed 15 minor faults, you're allowed zero major faults. So, for example, if at any point I had hit a curb with my tires (easy to do on narrow streets or when parking) or if I had even gone 1 or 2 mph over the speed limit, I could have received a major fault and failed. I knew this in advance, so I actually somewhat intentionally was a little bit wide in my left reverse maneuver, as I'd rather her give me a few minor faults for that instead of hitting the curb and completely fail.

Needless to say, after spending lots of money and time preparing for this moment, I was so relieved to pass and know that a driver's license would soon be in my hands!

Celebrating Holidays

A Guide to British Holidays

My kids went back to school today after a three-week Easter holiday. And by holiday, I mean vacation. In fact, that's the first thing Americans should know about British holidays. Here, a holiday means vacation or time away from work/school, not just the celebration of a religious or historically significant day.

You don't have to live here long to realize many Brits take their holidays very seriously. I love that about the culture here. I know far too many Americans who lose vacation time each year simply because they don't use it. Leisure time is precious, in my opinion, especially when you have children, so I love that people here respect the importance of that. Here are few things to know about "holidays":

According to a recent survey, the average British worker gets 26 paid days off per year. The average American worker gets 15. I see this play out on a personal level. When my husband took his expat assignment here, he had to keep his US vacation time, so he gets about two weeks less than his British co-workers do (including people who report to him, who have much less experience). Frustrating!

Bank Holiday weekends. If you're planning a trip to the UK, you'll want to pay attention to the bank holiday weekend schedule. It may mean that you'll face big crowds at various attractions, and it also might mean some businesses are closed.

Restaurants in particular fill up very quickly on those busy holiday weekends, so plan to book ahead at most places. Even the very casual pub in our village is usually fully booked on bank holiday weekends.

The school schedule is similar all over the country. Unlike in the US, where schools on the East Coast are on a much different schedule than schools in the Midwest, for example, the schools here run on roughly the same schedule all over the country. A big reason to take note of this: prices for popular family accommodations may shoot way up during the weeks that the schools are out. Center Parcs, for example, is a chain of popular family resorts. The price difference between a week's stay in June (when school is still in session) versus late July (when school is out) is over £600.

I've noticed that flight and train ticket prices change drastically around these weeks, too. And while it will mean there are more festivals and activities going on around the UK during these school holidays, again, there will be many more people visiting the various attractions, also. I visited the Natural History Museum in London when school was in session, and walked right in at 11 a.m. A few weeks later, I visited with my children when school was out and arrived 10 minutes before it opened, but still had to stand in line for about 30 minutes to get in.

So what is the school schedule here like? You may find some variation around the UK, but this is a rough outline:

- The school year begins the first or second week of September. This is called the autumn term. There is a week-long half-term break in mid-October, and the term ends in late

December for a 2-3 week break over the Christmas/New Year holiday.

- The spring term begins in January. There is a week-long half term break in mid-February. The term concludes around late March, with another 2-3 week break around Easter.

- The summer term begins in mid to late April. There is a week-long half-term break in late May (the week of the second May bank holiday weekend). The summer term concludes in mid-July.

What does a typical British holiday look like? Well, this surprised me a bit when I moved here. With continental Europe in their backyard, I assumed most Brits would spend their travel time and dollars visiting historic cities like Paris, Munich, Rome, etc. (In other words, the types of places Americans go to when visiting Europe.) Wrong. Brits actually vacation much like Americans: they hit the beach! A study by Skyscanner revealed that the top 10 most searched for destinations from UK airports were all popular beach areas in Spain, USA, Turkey and Portugal, as well as New York City and Geneva, Switzerland.

The travel we've been able to do on our "holidays" has been my absolute favorite thing about living here. We've seen quite a bit of England (Cornwall, London, Kent, Norfolk, the Lake District, the Peak District, Yorkshire, the Cotswolds, and more) and quite a bit of Europe, too.

Now when someone wishes you "happy hols" while you're on vacation here, you'll know what they're talking about!

Celebrating the 4th of July as Expats in England

One might think that England would rank as the most awkward place to be an American expat on the 4th of July. But having now celebrated three of those holidays here, I'd have to argue otherwise. No, it's not like being back "home," of course. But we've had some very memorable celebrations full of plenty of cheer.

How have we celebrated?

Year 1: We had only moved over a month prior. This was definitely one of the toughest days of our first year, at least in terms of homesickness. Someone from my son's school had invited us over for a play date in the morning, and she obviously had no idea it was a major holiday for our family. There was no mention of it. Which is completely understandable, but it just made me feel even lonelier for friends and family back home.

It fell on a weekday, so my husband was at work all day. Later that evening when he did get home, we had our kids decorate the backyard with little flags we had brought over, we cranked up some American music, and we used our grill for the first time since moving (all of our belongings have arrived only a few days prior). Then my mood lifted and we felt much better.

Year 2: When a couple of my husband's co-workers realized that the popular local event, Battle Proms, fell very close to the July 4 holiday, they organized a gathering for it.

It was so kind of them to plan something celebratory to help us take our minds off being away from home. And while the event was distinctively British, it also had a lot of the July 4 pomp and circumstance, like live music, fireworks, and picnic food. We had a great time and I'd love to go again.

Year 3: This year, July 4 fell on a Saturday, which was wonderful. A group of fellow American expats that I frequently socialize with organized a big party in one of our group's backyard. We rented a bounce house, set up kiddie pools, and had lots of our favorite July 4 foods from home (including American Flag Cake!). Our host decorated her home beautifully, everyone wore red, white and blue, and all the kids gathered together to sing God Bless America. It was a really special night.

Other observations?

The English actually don't begrudge Americans for celebrating Independence Day whatsoever. I've had many friends here wish us well on July 4. In fact, the hostess of our party is English (she's married to an American man) and she seemed to thoroughly enjoy pulling out all the stops to make it really festive for us. This year I noticed that our local radio station was taking requests for classic American songs that day, and there was a sale on American-style meats (like hot dogs) at the grocery store for people wanting to celebrate.

The only thing I can compare it to would be how Americans celebrate Cinco de Mayo and St. Patrick's Day, even though those are Mexican and Irish holidays.

That said, most people probably won't even realize it's a holiday unless they hear mention of it on the news or in some other way. It's always a bit jarring to me, to be scrolling Facebook one minute, with my newsfeed full of photos of people celebrating, and then leaving my house and having everything seem completely normal the next minute.

Finding ways to celebrate here actually makes July 4 more meaningful to me. When we lived in the US, celebrating came so easily. There were fireworks put on by our town or city. We'd likely be invited to a few gatherings, and could pick and choose what to do. Or maybe we'd have friends and family over to our house. Either way, there'd be plenty of people to enjoy the day with. We'd always have the day off from work, even if July 4 fell on a weekday. But when you're abroad, if you want to celebrate the day, you have to do it all yourself. And that actually makes it a lot more rewarding and memorable, as strange as that may sound.

I'll be back to writing about more things UK-focused next week, when I hope to share my favorite aspects of British summers.

Our First British Halloween: Do the British Celebrate?

As I'm sure you noticed, Halloween came and went last week. I got a lot of questions about how the holiday is celebrated here (or if it is celebrated at all). Here are a few of my observations from our first British Halloween.

Trick-or-treating is not the focus. Yes, kids do trick-or-treat here, but it is not as widely accepted as it is in the US. In other words, most kids where we live don't do it. I live on a fairly busy street, and we had one trick-or-treater that evening (and the weather was beautiful). Where I live, you indicate that your household is participating by putting a pumpkin by your door. I know several families who actually gave their neighbors some candy in advance to give to their kids in order to ensure there was a treat on hand for them.

The costumes are spookier and scarier. In the US, you can dress up as anything, from a baseball player to a beloved cartoon character to a princess. It's what the British would call "fancy dress." But here, the costumes are very much Halloween-focused: ghosts, skeletons, witches, etc.

The grocery stores are trying to make it a bigger deal than it actually is. You can tell that the stores are trying to capitalize on candy, decoration and other related purchases.

In fact, the only real decorations I saw for Halloween were in the stores themselves. No home had decorated door fronts, at least not in my village. I did spy the occasional carved pumpkin in a window.

There were several Halloween-themed events scheduled, particularly as a draw to get visitors to touristy places, like National Trust properties, farms, and theme parks. And I noticed this weekend that on Strictly Come Dancing, the popular ballroom dance competition television show, Halloween was the theme.

So how did we celebrate? We started the week by buying some pumpkins at the grocery store, which we painted. In the US, we would have definitely visited a pumpkin patch for that, but frankly I didn't have time to research if there was any place to go for that near us. Picking a couple up while I was at the store was much more convenient.

We chose not to trick-or-treat. I wasn't sure how popular or accepted it was in our village, and I wanted to respect the local culture here. In hindsight, I think we could have visited a few homes without much fuss. We will probably plan to do that next year. Frankly, it's not all the candy that I missed. It is the camaraderie with neighbors that I love about Halloween...your yearly excuse to knock on doors, say hello, and marvel at how much the kids have grown and changed since last year.

Instead, we went to a Halloween party at our village pub. It was lots of fun, with games, stories, pumpkin carving and cupcake decorating. My four-year-old, dressed as Spiderman, observed that the costumes were "really scary" and complained that he didn't get any candy.

Luckily, his grandmother back in the US sent him a package full of some of his favorites (and candy corn for my husband and me, which we don't have here). So we "treated" him when we got home from the party.

All in all, while it was different than how we would have celebrated in the US, it was an enjoyable day. And when asked by friends and family back home if they celebrate Halloween here, my answer remains, "sorta."

An American's First Bonfire Night

'Tis the season for holiday celebrations. Last week, I wrote about my first British Halloween. That same week, my fellow Anglotopia contributor Laurence reminisced about Guy Fawkes Night. You should read his post if you don't know much about the holiday's origin. I myself was gearing up for my first celebration of this uniquely British holiday. So I thought I'd share a few of my thoughts and observations from it.

It is sort of like the British 4th of July. Obviously, they don't celebrate July 4 here. (You'd be surprised by how many of my friends back home ask me this. Really? Duh.) But if you can picture what July 4 would be like if it was celebrated in early November, then you're pretty close: lots of fireworks (some organized, some "homemade" shows in people's gardens), big firework displays in the stores ready for purchase, bonfires to keep warm, adult beverages delicious, warm-you-to-the-core food....

I was confused by the name. Is it Guy Fawkes Night or Bonfire Night? For the most part, at least around where I live, it seemed to be more commonly referred to as Bonfire Night. Yet there was Guy Fawkes, a stuffed faux man perched on the top of the roaring fire at the party we attended. The kids were really excited to "watch him burn" as I heard one 8-year-old say. Pretty amusing.

I was also confused by the date. Festivities (and random fireworks) seemed to begin promptly on the evening of November 1. My town's celebration was November 2. My son's school's party, which we went to, was November 8. Yet the official holiday date is November 5. I suspect this is in part because the holiday fell on a Tuesday this year. And this is not a "get out of work and school" type of holiday, so naturally most celebrations were held on a weekend.

Overall, we really enjoyed the experience. Granted, we live in a quiet village, so the random fireworks that people let off in their backyards weren't much of an issue for us. I hear it can sound like a war battle in some areas in the evenings in early November. (No different than some areas of the US throughout July!) A few things I really appreciated about this tradition:

- Because it gets dark so early in the fall here, after the time change especially, the fireworks were let off at 7:15 at the party we attended. So enjoyable to let the kids participate in the highlight of the evening, without keeping them up hours after their typical bedtime.

- The camaraderie of the fire. I loved that everyone was basically forced to gather around the fire to keep warm. I had several really nice conversations that evening with total strangers. Had the cool night air not forced us to stand so close, perhaps I would have missed out on those interactions.

- Warm beverages like mulled wine, hot chocolate and tea, along with sausages straight off the grill. You can't just warm up from the outside via the fire. You've got to warm yourself from the inside by indulging in these treats, too. Or at least that's what I told myself.

- It was a nice excuse to venture outside in the evening, particularly in November. I know the winter nights will force us indoors most nights in the months ahead. It seemed fitting to give ourselves one last hurrah outside at this time of year.

Getting to experience another culture's traditions and holidays is one of the best aspects of being an expat. I suspect my family will carry a little bit of the spirit of Bonfire Night back home with us to the US in a few years. It'll be a great excuse to get our family and friends together, light a nice fire, and sip warm drinks each November. I'll probably leave the burning of Guy Fawkes to my British friends, though, in case the neighbors get suspicious.

Thanksgiving Across the Pond

Thanksgiving is probably my favorite holiday. I love the sentiment of expressing gratitude. I love that unlike some holidays, it's mostly centered on families spending quality time together, not on gifts, decorations and other areas of "excess" that sometimes overshadow Christmas. I love that most of my family has four straight days off from school and work (at least when we lived in the US). And what's not to love about the food?

Needless to say, spending the past three Thanksgivings in a country where it's not celebrated has often challenged me emotionally. I think I could live in England for decades and still be terribly homesick during the Thanksgiving week. But over the past few years, I've done my best to make the most of it and celebrate in a unique way.

Year 1: We weren't quite looped in yet with a big American expat community in our area of England the way we are now, so we had another American family that we had met over to celebrate on the Saturday following the holiday. (My husband goes to work all week, and my kids go to school, so celebrating on the weekend is the only way.)

It was the first time I had ever hosted a Thanksgiving, so it was exciting to know I could pull it off. We had a lovely evening. That Thursday was rather difficult, I remember spending a large part of the day crying and feeling very homesick.

Year 2: Last year, I took my youngest son (who didn't have nursery on Thursday) out for a pancake breakfast at an American-style diner, and then we came home and streamed the Macy's Thanksgiving Day Parade online. That weekend, I helped to organize a big expat celebration pitch-in dinner. We rented a village hall and about 30 of us gathered around tables and ate a huge feast. It was wonderful and very festive.

Year 3: This year, my in-laws came to visit two weeks prior to Thanksgiving week, so we cooked a Thanksgiving meal with them while they were here. It felt so great to have a family gathered around my table for the first time in years, even if we were a few days off on the actual holiday date. On Thursday of this week, I'm meeting some friends out for a holiday lunch (though I doubt it will be turkey we eat!). And we're once again having a large expat pitch-in meal at a village hall. We rented a hall with Wi-Fi so we could stream some American football during the afternoon/evening, so it should add another layer of "home" to the day.

As for the food, I'm usually able to find frozen turkeys the week prior to Thanksgiving at some of the larger grocery stores. I think they're mostly out for people who are buying ahead for their Christmas dinner (turkey is the common Christmas food here). My oven is actually too small to cook a full turkey, so I just cook a turkey crown.

My mom sends me the Pepperidge Farm stuffing mix a few weeks ahead of time so that I can recreate her stuffing recipe. I can always find cranberries and all the ingredients for mashed potatoes here, obviously.

We have a friend whose husband works on a military base so she's able to shop at the commissary and can get things like the fried onions that go on top of green bean casseroles. Pumpkin pie has to be made from scratch, and there's only one grocery store near me that sells canned pumpkin puree, so that classic dessert takes a little more effort, but can certainly be accomplished.

I'm also able to find Thanksgiving napkins on Amazon.co.uk (though they're certainly a bit more expensive and there's not much selection) for our pitch-in dinner. We'll print out some Thanksgiving-themed coloring pages for the kids to do during our celebration, and I always read our favorite Thanksgiving book to my kids that week. (*Spookley the Square Pumpkin*, if you need a recommendation!) And we sing the Thanksgiving turkey song my grandmother taught me as a kid. It's nice to pass along those traditions to my children and the fact that they're not learning about the holiday at school heightens my sense of responsibility to teach them all about it at home.

And yes, unfortunately Black Friday is becoming a tradition here as well. Personally, I hate what that crazy shopping day has become and I hate even more that so many people here in the UK seem to think that this is the event that dominates our Thanksgiving celebrations in the US. It's certainly not the case for my family and many others I know.

I had a good friend who was an expat in Asia tell me that she thinks the holidays she lived in the US eventually all blur together in her memory, but the holidays she spent abroad she'll always remember with perfect clarity.

I totally agree, and I'll always think of my Thanksgivings in England fondly. But I'm also glad that this might be my last one away from "home" in the US as we prepare for our move back in the coming months.

What You Can Learn About Britsh Culture from *Love Actually*

For as long as I can remember, the movie *Love Actually* has been my favorite holiday film. I'm guessing that if you're a reader of Anglotopia, you've probably seen it too. If you haven't, please stop reading this post and go watch it immediately.

I hadn't seen it in a few years, but on a recent trip into London I convinced my husband to watch it with me again. I couldn't be in London in December and not watch it...that would be criminal! But this time when I watched it, I couldn't help but notice all the accurate reflections of British culture, especially around Christmas, found in the movie. I'm not saying you'll actually see the Prime Minister kissing a staff member in a Nativity play, but here's a few things that are true to life here:

Christmas Number One

One of the funniest plot lines in the movie is old rocker Billy Mack's efforts to have his song be named the Christmas Number One. That's an actual title bestowed upon a popular holiday song each year here. Unfortunately for Billy, his song isn't climbing the charts in 2013.

The song for this year hadn't been named at the time I wrote this post, but my betting money is on Lily Allen's "Somewhere Only We Know." It's been quite popular this season, and is featured in the popular department store John Lewis' Christmas ad.

Critiquing Songs on Air

You may remember that when Mack's song debuted on the radio, the BBC broadcaster was quite critical of the tune after it played. I laugh when listening to the radio here because after playing a song, the broadcasters or hosts often share what they think of it, even if they don't really care for it. I've never heard a radio announcer be that honest in the US. Although I've yet to hear someone be so critical while the singer is in the room, like what happened to poor Mack in the film.

Importance of the Nativity

The performance of the school Nativity was the culmination of the movie, when many of the characters come together. From what I can tell, just about every primary school here puts on a Nativity play around the holidays. And it's very important. Moms and dads get out of work to attend, grandparents fill the school auditorium. A local radio station even had people calling in to share what part their sons or daughters have been cast as. There were not any lobsters or octopuses in my son's school's Nativity like are shown in the movie, but I was the proud parent of a little star this year.

Tea and Biscuits

Remember the scene when Hugh Grant, who plays the Prime Minister, wonders, "Who do you have to screw around here to get a cup of tea and a chocolate biscuit?" This probably comes as no surprise to anyone who is fond of British culture, but they really do love tea and biscuits here! I recently had a cultural faux pas when a repairman was working at my house on our broken heating system. I realized after he had been at my house for almost an hour that I hadn't offered him a cup of tea. I felt terrible but we had a nice laugh about how Americans don't think to do that.

Homecomings at Heathrow

The film ends with loads of families and friends meeting each other at Heathrow. The arrivals gate at this major international airport really is a magical place. I always love the diversity of the people you see there: people from all over the world, finally reunited with loved ones. I like to think about how long it's been since they last saw each other and how special this time must be for them. And now that I'm so far from my own friends and family, my appreciation for similar moments with the people I miss so greatly has only grown.

So those are just a few observations about the British way of life taken from scenes from my favorite Christmas movie.

How Christmas in the UK and US is Similar

Is everyone starting to feel the Christmas spirit? For my Dispatches posts this month, I'll be writing about all things Christmas. I didn't write much about the holiday last year; I was busy taking it all in and experiencing as much of the spirit of Christmas here in Great Britain as I could. But as I'm coming upon my second season now, I wanted to share some observations.

I'll start this week with the ways Great Britain and the US are similar in their celebration. Next week, I'll dive into a few differences. Then I'll share a few experiences that my family is hoping to check off the "bucket list" this year that we never had a chance to do last year. And finally, as the month of December comes to a close, I'll share my favorite things about spending Christmas in Great Britain. I hope you'll enjoy this Christmas series.

One of the reasons I'm not as homesick here during Christmas as I am at Thanksgiving is because the two countries actually celebrate and acknowledge the holiday quite similarly in many ways. This level of familiarity is comforting to me (although I love a lot of the differences and have embraced them, too!).

Christmas Trees

One of my favorite days of the holiday is when my family goes and selects our Christmas tree. We used to go to a farm in southern Indiana and cut one down in a field.

We haven't found a place like that near us (although I'm sure they exist), but we did still go to a farm and choose our tree from other pre-cut trees. "Fake" Christmas trees are also common here. And from what I've observed, the two countries decorate them similarly, too, with lights and ornaments that residents of either country would easily recognize. It's also common for towns and cities to have a large tree for the community.

Going to see Santa (or Father Christmas as the Brits call him)

If getting that photo of your child sitting on Santa's knee is central to marking another Christmas on the calendar for you, then you're in luck. Opportunities to meet the big guy are prevalent in both countries. Although if you're celebrating here in Great Britain, it's much more common to "book" an appointment to meet Santa (often called Father Christmas here), and popular events often sell out. For example, Harrods Santa's Grotto sold out weeks in advance. Last year, my kids saw Santa at a local farm that was doing a special Christmas event. This year, we're taking a steam train ride with Santa. For both, I reserved a couple of weeks in advance, so it does take some pre-planning.

Complaints about the season starting too soon and the commercialization of Christmas

If you thought it was just American stores that start putting out Christmas decorations in early October, you're wrong. It's just as common here. In fact, because Halloween isn't as popular here, and the lack of Thanksgiving, I sometimes feel the Christmas frenzy starts even earlier here.

And I frequently find myself in conversations about how commercialized Christmas has become, just as I did in the US.

Christmas Cards

It is quite popular here to exchange Christmas cards, just as it is in the US. In fact, I often find the British culture to be more into cards than the US, not exclusive to Christmas.

A Big Focus on Food

I remember discussing what we might eat for our Christmas celebration with my family weeks ahead of time. It's similar here, too. In fact, most people order their large cuts of meat in advance from the grocery store or butcher to ensure they get what they want. The food itself is somewhat similar: turkey is common, as is ham or beef roasts. Sides differ somewhat, as roast potatoes and Brussels sprouts seem more prevalent here than in the US. I'll talk more about popular British Christmas foods in upcoming posts this month. But regardless, if Brits or Americans sat down to a Christmas meal on either side of the pond, I don't think either would feel too out of place.

There are plenty of other similarities, these are just a few that seemed important to share!

A Few Ways Christmas in the UK is different from the USA

Last week, I wrote about ways that the Christmas holiday is celebrated similarly in the US and the UK. This week, I'd like to tackle a few of the differences. Before anyone gets upset, **I'm leaving off a few key differences**, only because I'm being a little cheeky since I plan to write about them in my next two posts (things we're trying for the first time this holiday, and my favorite aspects of spending the holidays here in the UK). So be patient (something I'm telling my kids each morning when they ask if it's Christmas yet. 'Tis the season)!

Boxing Day

I vividly remember my first Christmas after graduating from college. It seemed so cruel that I had to go to work the day after Christmas. I was accustomed to having several weeks off when I was a student. But not so here, as the 26th of December is a holiday here in addition to Christmas. I'm mostly just an observer of the tradition, but I've asked around as to how people celebrate. It seems to me that it's celebrated pretty casually. I know lots of families host "open house" style gatherings, where friends and family pop over for a visit and leftovers from the formal meal the day prior are often served. And much like the 26th of December in the US, shopping is quite common too.

Christmas Shopping Hours

Speaking of shopping, if you're the type of American that likes to hit the mall or Target late into the evening to get your shopping done, you'd be out of luck here. My husband and I were laughing because we kept getting flyers in the mail from our closest mall advertising their "late night Thursday hours." The mall was open until 8 p.m. on the Thursdays leading up to Christmas. Malls in the US are usually open until 9 or 10 p.m. every day of the week, year-round. Late night shopping hours would probably be midnight. I find that I do more online shopping here, especially at Christmas. I have my kids with me during the hours of the day when shops are open, so if I want to keep gifts a secret from them it's my easiest option.

School Nativities

Having a holiday performance or show of some kind at schools is common in both countries. But every child I know here in the UK (so mostly just in my area of England) between the ages of 4-7 have participated in a school Nativity play (including my oldest son). Just last week the local radio station was having parents call in to share what role their child was performing in the school Nativity. It seems to be a much bigger deal here in the UK. One funny story is that my son's Nativity theme this year was Christmas Around the World. One group of children represented the USA. They wore jeans, t-shirts and tennis shoes (called trainers here) and sang a gospel-style Christmas song. My son was up on stage and mouthed to us, "That was USA!" As if we couldn't tell!

Decorating Exterior of Homes

While it's common to have a Christmas tree in both countries, you'll see far fewer exterior decorations on homes here in the UK. For example, my village has about 200 homes. Only two have Christmas lights up as of this week (which is one more than last year!). I've heard anecdotally that this seems to be changing, and that Christmas lights are beginning to become more popular, but it's still nowhere near the level it is in the US. We no longer put the kids in the car on a December evening to drive around looking at lights on homes like we did in America. But, Christmas lights are popular in town and city centers or shopping areas. The town closest to my village has lovely lights on its high street. And obviously London has some spectacular areas for lights and decorations.

Christmas = Closed

Here in the UK, everything shuts down on Christmas Day. I'm not sure you'd even find a gas station open that day (maybe just those off the major motorways). Movie theatres, trains, the London Tube, grocery stores, absolutely everything is closed. Personally, I love that. It means that everyone can be with their families or loved ones, aside from necessary emergency and medical personnel. However, I went to the grocery store on the 23rd of December last year to pick up a few last minute items we needed, and it was absolute chaos in there. I've never seen a store so crowded in all my life. This year, I'll definitely plan ahead and try to avoid the store several days in advance!

British Christmas Traditions We're Trying for the First Time

It was difficult our first year in the UK to find the time to fit in all the British Christmas traditions we wanted to experience in just one holiday season. Inevitably there were a few things we didn't quite get around to doing or trying last year. So in 2014, we've made it our goal to try to check those remaining things off our list. Here are a few things we'll be doing for the first time this year.

A Pantomime

The fact that we didn't get a chance to see a pantomime was one of my biggest disappointments last year. A pantomime, or panto for short, is a family-friendly musical show put on at theatres all over the country. They're often based on fairy tales or other well-known stories. These shows are known for having lots of slapstick comedy, audience participation, even gender-crossing actors. We took our sons to see a Jack and the Beanstalk pantomime last weekend and it was one of my favorite experiences. Mostly because my kids absolutely loved it and are still talking about it a full week later.

A Proper Christmas Pudding

Last year I kept seeing these wrapped up packages all over the grocery store, beginning in November, proclaiming to be Christmas pudding.

I wasn't quite sure what that meant, since pudding here generally refers to dessert of any kind. So what made something a Christmas pudding? The fact that it was wrapped in several layers of packaging meant that I couldn't even really see what it was. For whatever reason, I never ended up purchasing one to give it a try, and our Christmas passed by without that. This year, I vow to give it a whirl. From what I can tell, people here tend to have a love/hate relationship with Christmas pudding. I'll let you know what I think once I've tried it.

Victorian Christmas

I love the emphasis on history and tradition in this country. My oldest son is studying the Victorian period in school, and I had the chance to chaperone his class trip for a day of celebrating Christmas as they did in Victorian times. We sang carols, made Christmas wreaths with leaves, branches and holly as they did in those days, dressed the Christmas tree, warmed ourselves around a fire, and even sat through a school lesson taught by a very strict teacher. We all had to dress in Victorian-style clothes and it was great fun. A nice way of experiencing a taste of historic British Christmas traditions. We may try to visit a Victorian-themed Christmas market this weekend so that my husband and youngest son get a taste of the fun, too.

London on Christmas Eve

Last year, we spent a weekend in London in early December. It was wonderful, but I had wished we had spent more time doing

Christmas activities and less time hitting the tourist attractions we could have visited any time of year. Since one of the harder aspects of being an expat is that we don't have family to celebrate the holidays with and the days can feel a bit lonely, this year I planned for us to go into London on Christmas Eve for the day. We have no agenda other than to wander around and admire the decorations and venture into a few of London's iconic shops for some gifts. Most of the museums and sites will be closed, so we won't even feel tempted to play the role of tourist, and can instead focus on savoring the holiday spirit in one of the most exciting cities in the world. I can't wait.

A Carol Service

I've attended carol concerts in the US, but not one here. Our village church has a service this weekend and we're hoping to make it so that we can experience that here. Nothing puts me in the Christmas spirit like music. Our village church is beautiful, so I'm sure it'll be a really special setting.

My Favorite British Christmas Traditions So Far

This is my last in a series of posts about Christmas in Great Britain this month. I always like to end on a high note, so here are a few of my favorite British Christmas traditions.

Mince Pies

I actually thought there might be meat in mince pies before I had my first one. Which isn't that strange, for two reasons: ground beef is called mince here, and savory pies are far more common than the sweet pies most Americans think of when we think of pie. But mince pies are the exception here, a pastry crust full of dried fruits and a sweet, dark syrup. I think they're so delicious with a cup of tea on a cold evening.

Crackers

Crackers are paper decorations, where you pull each end and they explode with a little bang. Inside, you'll find a little treat of some kind. Almost always, there's a paper hat along with some other token or trinket and maybe a little joke written on paper. The quality of whatever is inside will vary depending on how much you spend on your crackers. (I've seen boxes of crackers for as much as 10 pounds. I've only ever bought the cheap boxes!) My children love these, and I think they're a fun little way to add a bit of humor to your Christmas dinner. I sent some to my mom so that my family back home in America can have a touch of Great Britain at their Christmas gathering this year.

Saying Happy Christmas and Father Christmas

I love that Happy Christmas and Father Christmas are a bit more common here than Merry Christmas and Santa (although those are typical too, and no one will look at you strange if you say those things, take it from me). They both sound a little old fashioned and classic to me, and I think they're very charmingly British.

London Around the Holidays

For a long time, I've dreamed of spending a December weekend in New York City. Seeing the tree at Rockefeller Center, ice skating, all the city sights decorated for the season.... When we moved here and I realized London was practically at my doorstep, I've been able to experience the magic of Christmas in one of the best cities in the world. Probably just as good as spending it in New York City. So in some ways, it's been a dream fulfilled.

Christmas Advertisements

Most of the major department and grocery stores here release special advertisements (called adverts here) during the holidays. I suppose this is true in the US, too, but here these commercials tug at your emotional heartstrings and are so beautifully crafted they almost feel like little movies.

My favorites this year were Sainsbury's (some didn't like the commercialization of this actual event during World War I, but I personally loved it) and John Lewis.

I've really been enjoying your comments about what you love about Christmas in Great Britain. To me, Christmas is first and foremost about being with your family, and so that has been difficult for me being so far away from them the past two years. But I truly do appreciate this opportunity to experience the holiday season in such a special place and writing about it this month has helped to capture that sentiment for me.

British Culture

My Favorite British Expressions

One of the most charming aspects of living here is hearing and learning the unique turns of phrase or expressions people use here. I know it's one aspect of British culture that many Americans are fascinated with, also. So here are a few of my favorites. I'd love to know which expressions you've heard and what you love about them.

A Right Charlie

When I came to the UK on a housing visit before we moved here, I was chatting with our estate agent (Realtor) and he described someone as "a right Charlie." I had to Google it when I was back in our hotel to find out if he was complimenting this person or not. Turns out, he was calling the man a fool. It was one of those first few eye-opening experiences, when you realize how different the two cultures actually are at times, despite the common language.

Horses for Courses

I wish I could remember when I first heard this expression. It basically means you should choose the right person for the right job. I later did a bit more research into it, and learned from Wikipedia that it stems from horse racing, as in a horse will perform best on a racecourse that it is well suited for.

Bob's your uncle and Fanny's your aunt.

I heard this while watching a Jamie Oliver cooking show. He was trying to show how easy it was to finish off the dish he was making, and as he scattered the last of the seasoning on the plate, he said this.

I laughed for a long time. And then, of course, I had to Google what point he was trying to make. It basically means "and that's it, all done, all is right." Similar to saying "voila!" in French. I'd love to incorporate it into my own speech but I just think this is one of those phrases you can't pull off with an American accent.

Right as Rain

Only in a country where it often rains could this become a common expression. It's typically used when something is now perfectly fine, as in, I had a cold for a few days, but now I'm right as rain.

Bits and Bobs

My husband was watching a football match (soccer game for you Americans) and one of the reporters was interviewing players in the locker room before the match. He said, "Fellas, don't forget to hide your bits and bobs, we're broadcasting live right now." I felt a bit immature about it, but I must have laughed for several minutes. Bits and bobs usually just means an assortment of things, but I'm sure we can all figure out what this reporter was referring to in this instance.

My Guilty Pleasure British Television Shows

It's no surprise to anyone familiar with British culture that this is a country known for a sharp sense of humor. In fact, it might be one of the greatest sources of British pride among the people here. Funny television shows are a great example of this, and I have a few favorites. These are the types of shows I love to watch after a busy, stressful day because I completely check out of whatever might be bothering me, and instead spend an hour laughing my head off.

An Idiot Abroad

Many Americans will be familiar with comedian Ricky Gervais. But do you know his best friend, Karl Pilkington, and his *The Office* co-writer Stephen Merchant? This show is based around the travels of Karl, and his experiences being sent on one adventure after another around the globe. The funniest scenes occur when he phones Ricky and Stephen to complain about the various crazy things they have set up for him, from sumo wrestling to bug-infested hotels. It is almost like a documentary, in the sense that Karl has no idea what's in store for him, and you get his true reactions to foreign cultures somewhat unfiltered. Picture the home videos that your least cultured friend on a trip around the world would make, and that pretty much captures it.

Gogglebox

The concept of this show sounds completely ridiculous and boring. The producers set up a stationary camera in several households, which then films them while they watch television to get their reactions. That's it. So simple. But they have found the most hysterical people, and how they each respond to various shows that they watch has me laughing out loud constantly. My favorite *Gogglebox* "characters" (though these are just regular people) are Leon and June, the older couple frequently featured on the show. Leon sitting back in his recliner chair and spewing out all sorts of opinions always makes me think of my dad.

The Graham Norton Show

Graham Norton is a popular presenter here, somewhat comparable to David Letterman, as he hosts this weekly late night show on BBC One. I think Graham is very witty and funny, but my favorite part of this show is how relaxed the various celebrities that he interviews are. This is especially true of the American celebrities, who often seem very tight-lipped on US programs. They really open up on Graham's show and "let their hair down." Perhaps it's the cocktails they drink while on air?

8 Out of 10 Cats

My husband got me hooked on this show. I think I was confused by the title of it and never bothered to watch it when scrolling through the channels at night.

It's a panel-style show that has two teams. On each team is at least one professional comedian and a couple of other celebrities. The host, Jimmy Carr, quizzes the panelists about popular topics in the news that week and their thoughts about those issues.

It reminds me a little bit of the old show that Drew Carrey hosted called *Whose Line Is It Anyway?* (Which is, of course, a show that started in the UK.)

Unexpected Moments of Culture Shock

Before we moved to England a few months ago, I had traveled to Europe enough to be prepared for some of the more obvious, expected differences. I knew I wouldn't get much ice in my drink at a restaurant. I knew I'd sometimes I have to pay a few coins to use a public toilet. I knew air conditioning was rare.

But as we settled into life here, a few differences have come as a surprise to me. Or they simply were not something I had thought much about. So I'm keeping a record of all my unexpected moments of culture shock and plan to share these from time to time.

Nursery Rhymes

Taking my two boys to storytime each week at a local children's center has been one of my favorite traditions here in England. But on our first day, I was a bit taken aback by the difference in nursery rhymes. Some were new to me altogether (like "Wind the Bobbin Up"), others were different variations of those we did know (like "Twinkle Twinkle Chocolate Bar" instead of "Twinkle Twinkle Little Star"). We have really enjoyed learning new songs and the British twists on old favorites. It reminds me of why we wanted to provide this type of opportunity for our kids to begin with—the chance to see how kids live in other parts of the world.

Writing a Check

Check is more than just spelled differently here (cheque). It also looks quite different. So when we received our booklet of cheques, my husband and I both scratched our heads. A cheque basically requires the same information you'd provide on a US check, just in different spots.

Drive-thrus

I knew American fast food establishments were somewhat plentiful abroad (For better or for worse, that's a topic for another post!), so I thought I'd just be adjusting to having a drive-thru pickup window on the other side of the car. Instead, I'm learning that drive-thrus are a very rare thing here altogether. I'm not much of a fast food eater, but I do like to indulge in the occasional fountain soda, and when I do, I prefer not to drag my kids out of the car to go inside. But I hardly ever find a drive-thru, even on highway exits. (Which is probably a good thing, as it stands between me and a large Diet Coke.)

Shirts Optional

No, I'm not referring to topless beaches. But I have found that it seems to be culturally acceptable for men to take their shirts off on hot days here. Since we've had a warm summer (by British standards) I've seen quite a bit of it. Construction workers, dads at the park, even men just walking down a street in the center of town. All without their shirts. In America, you'd typically only see men without shirts at the beach, pool, or mowing their yard. I just hope they're all applying lots of sun cream!

Charming Bits of British Culture You've Never Heard Of

Anyone who has an interest in British culture (and even those that don't) have probably heard about some of the more common traditions here, like being offered a cup of tea everywhere you go and being told to "mind the gap" (or your head, or the step, etc.). But I've been completely taken by some that I wasn't aware of before we moved here a few months ago. I hope to share some of my favorites as time passes.

Here are a few observations I've made so far:

Lending Libraries

I think this is my favorite, perhaps because I use them frequently. Occasionally, at a shop's entrance or exit, you'll find a little stack of used books along with a jar for spare change. You're invited to pick up a book and keep it, as long as you drop a few coins in the bucket (usually 50 pence is suggested) for charity. You're also encouraged to share any used books you'd be happy to part with for the next person. My village shop has one, but I also see them at big box stores like Homebase. I think it's equally adorable, generous, and practical. I've picked up a few good reads this way.

The Courtesy Wave

One of the more challenging aspects of driving here (I'll save the rest for a separate post!) is that many two-way streets only have enough space for one car at a time.

So you're often stopping in the middle of the street to give the car coming at you space to get through. The accepted practice is to give the driver who stopped a wave.

Calling Children "Cheeky"

This is one I often hear, given the naughty nature of my two little boys. I love when people can accept children's abundant energy and laugh off some of the crazy behavior with a simple, "What a cheeky little boy!" Kids will be kids the world over; leave it to the British to have such a charming term for it.

"Anti-social Behavior"

Speaking of charming terms, guess what public intoxication is called here? Anti-social behavior. The first time I heard it, I couldn't fathom it as a way of describing what are typically lewd acts! And you might even argue that a few too many pints at the pub is quite social, not anti-social. Ha!

Signing Off With "xx"

Perhaps this is new with the dawn of social media, but all of my British friends and acquaintances sign off messages with "xx." It reminds me of what I might have written in a note to a boyfriend in middle school: xoxo. I think it's a lovely little way of showing someone a bit of written affection.

What are some interesting British cultural observations that you've made? Let us know in the comments!

Things That the British Think Are True About Americans

Over the course of my nearly four months living here in Great Britain, I've been able to learn a few generalities that British people make or say about Americans. Mostly, these make me chuckle, often because they're far from true. I enjoy thinking about how and why these observations have become common here. (My hunch is that it is primarily from the influence of American television shows.) And don't worry Americans, I do my best to disprove those that are false.

We eat Lucky Charms for breakfast.

This one caught me very much by surprise. Someone was telling me about a store nearby that carries a lot of American products (mostly food) that you can't find in the typical grocery stores here. She mentioned I'd be able to get Lucky Charms, the sugary, Leprechaun-themed cereal. "Isn't that what Americans eat for breakfast?" she asked. I gently explained that while some young children (and maybe a few college students) eat this cereal occasionally, it's certainly not the common breakfast for most Americans.

We all have huge yards and outdoor swimming pools.

There's definitely a bit of truth to this one. (I'm sure, on average, the yards in America are much larger than the gardens in Great Britain.

And I'm also certain there are far more outdoor swimming pools in those big yards in the US.) One person told me they think we all have pools because every American family on the television show *Super Nanny* has one.

It's always warmer in America than in Great Britain.

In the summer, most of the US is likely to be experiencing warmer days than you find here. (And don't get me started on the complaints about the heat here. It's actually a big pet peeve of mine.) But in the winter, much of the US is colder than you find here. I experienced this last winter, when during my housing visit a couple of inches of snow threatened to shut everything down and life almost came to a standstill. All this for a little bit of snow that anyone living in the northern half of the US wouldn't even bother putting snow boots on for!

We've been everywhere in the US (especially NYC).

I enjoy talking to British people I meet about places they've been to in the US. They're often excited to share those travel experiences with me. And I'm always thankful that I'm relatively well-traveled around the US because they almost always assume I've been to those places also. This is particularly true about New York City. I know many, many Americans who have never been to New York, but so many British people I meet ask me what NYC is like before even asking if I've been there. (I'm glad I have, both because it's an amazing city, but also so I can answer some of their questions about it!)

We don't have a good sense of humor.

There's definitely a difference between British humor and American humor. But I find many British people and entertainers quite funny. Some of the television shows here leave me in stitches with their sarcasm and good humor. But I've been asked point blank if I find anything here funny or if I understand jokes. We might not be as funny as Ricky Gervais, but most Americans can have a good laugh, too!

Strange British Things I've Had to Google Since Moving Here

I'm coming up on my 6-month anniversary of our move to England. I laugh now at some of the most basic things that confused me when we first moved here, and yet I still find myself puzzled by certain cultural differences. I thought it might be fun to take a look at some of the things I've had to turn to the internet for help with over the past few months as we settled into daily life here. Here's a small snapshot of my Google search history.

What's a conker?

Throughout the fall season, I kept reading about "playing conkers" or encouraging your kids to find conkers. When my son came home from school talking about doing an art project with conkers, I figured I'd better get a handle on this. Apparently it's the seed from a chestnut tree, and also a popular children's game here. (I'm guessing Brits moving to the American Midwest probably end up googling "what's cornhole" for a very similar reason!)

Will they sing "God Save the King"?

Upon the birth of the Royal Baby, I got to wondering what happens to the national anthem when a man sits on the throne. Turns out, it will change to "God Save the King," naturally. I've just never heard that version, given how long the Queen has been running the show.

What is Pudsey Bear?

A few weeks ago, the whole country rallied around the charitable cause of Children in Need. There were school fundraisers, coffee mornings, and nationally televised telethons all to raise money for various children's charities. My son's nursery encouraged the kids to dress up like Pudsey Bear one morning. I had no idea who or what it was, but it is the charity's mascot, pictured above. (Sort of like Smokey the Bear represents the prevention of forest fires in the US.)

Where is Wayne Rooney from?

My husband and I are big sports fans, so we've tried to watch plenty of football matches. (Note that I've learned enough to know not to call it soccer!) Wayne Rooney is one of the most popular players here, and we were watching an interview with him after a match. We think it's fun to try to distinguish the various accents you find around the UK and his was particularly unique. Turns out he's from Liverpool.

How do I cook a frozen pork pie?

I've had to research a lot of stuff about cooking since moving here. Converting Fahrenheit to Celsius, ounces to grams, etc. When we first moved here, someone gave us a pork pie as a gift. I didn't want it to go bad, but I also didn't really know what it was, so I put it in the freezer. Just the other day, I was scrambling to come up with something to make for dinner and saw it in the freezer. We now know all about pork pies and how delicious they are, but I didn't have a clue as to how to turn it from the ice blob that it was into a tasty meal.

I can't help but wonder what expats did before the invention of Google. It certainly makes my life easier on a daily basis, providing everything from postal codes to nearby parks so that I can find my way there, to figuring out which stores ship to the UK.

More Charming British Traditions

This country really is as charming as I imagined it would be, and the longer I live here, the more I notice it. So here are a few more traditions that I love. I should point out that some of these may be a regional custom to where I live in England. I've traveled a bit around the UK so far, but certainly don't know what's considered common everywhere around the country.

Bunting

I absolutely adore bunting, the little fabric triangles hanging from string. I've seen it strung across the high street of market towns, on houses (strung between windows), used as decoration in a village hall for a party, and frequently in store windows. Whenever I see it hung somewhere, I think it adds such a festive feel and it always makes me smile. There's even a park near us that frequently hangs bunting between the trees all around the playground. When we move back, I'd love to use bunting in some way to decorate in my home, as a way of bringing a little bit of Britain back with us.

Shortening Words

I think this happens from time to time in the US too, but I notice it more here. I often see in print or hear people say "pudds" instead of pudding (which here means dessert in general, not just the creamy Jello-style pudding we're used to in America), "mo" for moment, and "brill" for brilliant.

Houses with Names

One of the more confusing things for me when we first moved here was trying to find someone's house when all they supplied me with was a name, not a house number. It's quite common here in villages for a house to have a name and not a house number. Sometimes the name is based on what the house might have originally been used for (like "Old School House"). Other times it might just be the ancestral name handed down over the generations. Or sometimes it's just a simple title like "The Cottage." In larger towns or cities, the houses may still be named but it will also be accompanied by a house number so as to avoid confusion. My house has a house number but is also called "The Chimes." I have no idea why!

"That's lovely."

I knew British people used the term "lovely" a lot prior to moving here. I guess I just didn't realize quite how much. It is a rare occasion when I pay for something and the cashier doesn't say, "That's lovely," when I hand over cash or insert my credit card into the machine.

Lambing Season in Britain

Since we have not yet lived in Great Britain for a full year, we're still experiencing each season here for the first time. I've always loved the changes in season, and never more so than this year, getting to see what makes it unique in this part of the world.

I often laugh to my friends back in the US that I've seen more sheep since moving to England than I did in my previous 32 years of life. I'm truly not exaggerating, I had no idea sheep were this prevalent anywhere, other than Ireland, maybe. And each spring, the lambs make their way into the world. (I read that more than 16 million lambs are born in the UK each year!) It's every bit as adorable as you might imagine, and fortunately, there are several ways to take part or observe, even for non-farmers like me.

First of all, just driving around the countryside here is a lot more fun right now. I pass at least a dozen fields with sheep no matter what direction I head when leaving my house, and it's been so interesting to see the lambs out in the fields with the ewes (their mothers). I first noticed them last week and can't wait to watch them grow older over the next few months.

There are several farms near my home that are open to the public and definitely cater to tourists. I took my youngest son (2 years old) to one of those places last week so that we could see the lambs up close. Much to our surprise, we were even handed a bottle of warm milk and a lamb to feed ourselves.

My son was too afraid, but I really enjoyed it and he liked watching me do it. Our lamb was quite an aggressive eater, and he sucked down the enormous bottle in about 2 ½ minutes! These farms all have lambing shows and special events that allow visitors to get a close-up and hands on experience.

For those of you not privy to this type of experience, I captured a very short video of a few of the lambs and ewes at the farm we visited (link below). (I'm very much an amateur when it comes to video, but I wanted everyone to get a little taste of just how cute they are.)

My older son (4 years old) will be joining his classmates on a field trip to a private farm this week. I'm hoping he'll get a chance to bottle-feed a lamb. (I've already talked to him about being brave and not missing this opportunity like his brother!) He spent some time last week at school learning about lambs and the birth process, as they're hoping a lamb might be born while they visit the farm. I'm sure that will leave quite an impression on him!

There's even a television show here called *Lambing Live* that airs on BBC 2. I missed this season's premiere last week, but hope to catch some of the episodes as the show progresses. The hosts follow a different sheep farmer and their family each year throughout the process of raising sheep, including the most important time of year, when the lambs are born.

I hope to learn a lot more about this agricultural industry in the months and years ahead, as it surrounds my new home and is such an important fabric of the community in the rural areas of the UK.

Things British People Take More Seriously Than Americans

Over the past 11 months as an American expat living in Great Britain, I've had a chance to observe some differences in personal habits and preference once you've crossed the pond. So here are a few things that Brits take more seriously than Americans (in my opinion, at least).

Ironing

I've had more conversations about ironing since moving here than I ever had living in America. To be honest, I do not iron unless it's an absolute fashion emergency. In fact, we've yet to even purchase an iron here. (Most electrical devices that have a heating element cannot be used on the different voltage system here.) Yet I hear people say they need to catch up on their ironing on the weekend, or that they iron their duvet covers. Now I realize that some Americans might iron more than I do, and some British people may never iron. But there does seem to be a difference in culture on this bit of housekeeping. The only American I know who ironed bedding was my grandmother, and even she stopped doing it at some point.

Dining Out

Friends back home in the US have asked me if people here eat out as much as Americans do.

My general observation would be that no, they don't. But I think the real difference is that Americans often eat out for convenience (don't feel like cooking, running around between commitments, no time to grocery shop, etc.), while British people eat out more for the pleasure of it. And therefore, they take the experience seriously. (It's also, generally speaking, more expensive to dine out here.) Just take a skim through Trip Advisor reviews to get a taste of the things people complain about (or compliment) when dining out. Many of them make me chuckle. I'll probably do a more complete post on the differences in dining out here in a future post, so stay tuned.

Gardening

Certainly, gardening is a popular hobby in both countries, but I find that gardening is an interest of a far wider range of people here than in the US, even if it just means they dabble a little in their own yards (called a garden here, so it gets a little confusing). One of my favorite discoveries since moving here has been garden centers. They're large stores that sell anything from seeds to pots to patio furniture (and often clothes, toys, books, live fish, and more!). For my American readers, these centers are kind of like a combination of Lowe's/Home Depot and your favorite specialty nursery. One of the reasons I frequent them is that some of them have cafes and play areas for kids, which my children enjoy. Visiting famous and historical gardens is also a popular outing in the spring and summer months here, and my son has had entire lessons at school based on various plants that are currently in bloom (like snowdrops and daffodils). I've learned a lot about gardening since moving here.

The vessel for their "cuppa"

It's already common knowledge that British people love a good, hot beverage (tea, obviously, but also coffees and hot chocolate too). But what did surprise me is how opinionated they are about their mug. I've overheard so many conversations about how awful it is to be served tea in a paper to-go cup, or that a mug was too small (or too big). My husband reports that everyone in his office has their go-to preferred mug in the shared kitchen. And I must admit, I'm a convert to this attitude. I was back in the US briefly to visit friends and family, and made my cup of tea in the hotel lobby with a Styrofoam cup. I nearly spit it out!

A Guide to My Favorite British House Hunting TV Shows

This might anger a few of the loyal Anglotopia readers, who love their British "telly," but I don't watch much television here. It's actually just a function of lifestyle: as a freelance writer who also stays home with my children, I often spend my evenings writing and working instead of watching shows.

But one type of television show that I find myself drawn to (or turning on even when my kids are around because they think it's boring and pay no attention to it) is house hunting shows. Perhaps it's because I can relate to the people on the show, searching for a home in the UK as my husband and I did a year ago. For the American readers, these are similar to watching the popular show *House Hunters International*. So I thought I'd share a few of my favorites of these shows.

Location, Location, Location

This is by far my favorite. I adore the hosts, Phil Spencer and Kirstie Allsopp. They're a property expert team that have great chemistry. (I actually thought they were married at first!) They host several other shows, both together and individually, and are quite popular over here. I also love the way they talk to the guests who appear on the show, many of whom don't have a realistic concept of what their money will buy in the location they want. The show could actually be called *Compromise, Compromise, Compromise*.

A Place in the Sun: Home or Away

All the guests on this show are searching for a home far away from where they currently live. Sometimes it's just as a vacation home, others are looking to move further away permanently. This show is fascinating because the guests have to make a fundamental (and often life-changing) decision: do they buy a home somewhere further away in the UK, or do they move abroad? For example, in the most recent episode I watched, a family was looking for homes in Pembrokeshire, Wales, and also in southwest France. They chose France. It's also interesting to see what their money buys them in the UK vs. Abroad.

Escape to the Country

I personally relate to this show the most, as my family found our own home "in the country" here. Most of the guests on this show are looking to move to a more rural part of the UK from their urban dwelling. They are looking at some of the same types of properties I saw when we were house hunting. In fact, one recent episode was filmed near my house. It's always fun to see what types of features guests are looking for. Some are adamant about a large garden, or period features, or proximity to public transport to ease their commute. One added bonus feature of this show is the segment that they do on the local area. The host (which varies) experiences something unique to that town, like seeing how a local food specialty is made, taking a tour of a historic property or attraction, etc. I enjoy learning about the various areas of the UK where they film.

Grand Designs

I have a bit of a love/hate relationship with this show. The premise is that the host (Kevin McCloud) follows the progress of people who undertake insanely ambitious housing projects. I've watched people convert everything from ruined castles to water towers to airplane hangars into immaculate and stunning homes. It's amazing to watch. And yet so frustrating—some of these guests take decades to complete the projects, and put themselves in financial ruin to do it. The host can be a bit over my head, as well. Perhaps it's just my lack of knowledge about design and architecture, but he's a little snobby for my tastes. Either way, it's the type of show that once I start watching, I'm hooked and have to see it until the end to know what happens. And yet sometimes I'm screaming at the television for the duration of the show!

My Family's Favorite Brit Foods

I plan to write a lot more about the food here in the UK. As time passes, we discover more and more about the cuisine and various foods unique to each region of the country and I'm excited to share that with you (and hear more about what you love).

For now, I thought I'd start by asking each member of my family what their favorite foods are.

My two-year-old: This kid can't get enough **Heinz baked beans**. I'll confess that I don't really care for baked beans myself, and so he had never had them prior to moving here. But since they are often the side item with a kid's meal in a restaurant, he sampled them quite early in our time living here. And we discovered that he loves them! I now regularly serve them to him for lunch (although they're traditionally more of a breakfast food here). At 40 pence for a small can (approximately $.60), it's such a cheap and relatively healthy way to make him happy.

My five-year-old: One of the hardest adjustments for our oldest son when moving abroad was the food. He was quite picky and didn't care for much of the food here at first. (I actually think it was less about the food, and more his way of processing all of the big changes in his life.)

Starting school and eating school lunch every day changed all that for the better, though. He now adores **fish and chips** (among lots of other British staples). They serve it almost weekly at his school, and he can't wait to tell me when I pick him up that he got to eat it for lunch.

He loves to order it out at restaurants, too. It's a staple on kids' menus. Sure, it's not the healthiest of foods, but he's a skinny kid and could use a few extra calories!

My husband: While we really miss good Mexican food, it has helped to discover how great **Indian and Thai curry dishes** are. Curry takeaway shops are about as common in the UK as Starbucks is in the US. A Friday night tradition in our house is to order some of this (and give me a break from cooking). I can't really handle spicy food (fortunately many dishes are mild), but my husband loves the hot stuff. We're on a quest to learn more about Indian food in particular since it's so prevalent here. (In fact, stay tuned... we're taking an Indian cooking class and I'll report more on the experience here soon.)

Me: One of the biggest food surprises to me has been how fantastic **the local cheese** is in the UK. Having spent very little time in the UK prior to moving here, I just never realized how tasty British cheeses are. I now regularly buy blocks of nice cheese each week at our local market. Even the sliced cheese you buy at the grocery store, perfect for sandwiches, tastes incredible. I don't know how I'll go back to eating American cheese. I think it will taste so flavorless to me! I'll write a post in the future describing some of my favorite varieties.

There are so many more foods we love here; this is just a start! I'll be writing a lot more about food in the coming weeks and months.

What Surprised Me When I Returned Briefly to the US

I'm back! After taking the month of August off from the Dispatches from England column, I've now got a fresh list of ideas for content to carry through the next few months that I'm excited to write about and share. But tops on my list is definitely some reflections from the three weeks I spent back in the US this summer. It had been over a year since my family had spent a great length of time here (my husband returns for business occasionally and I spent one whirlwind 48 hours in Chicago in February). Needless to say, we made lots of cultural observations that I'll be reporting on.

One of the things I was keen to pay attention to was what immediately jumped out at me. So I'm sharing things that surprised me or caught me off guard about being back in the US during our first 24 hours there.

I was Freezing Indoors

Having spent the last year largely out of air conditioned buildings (it's somewhat unheard of in homes here in the UK, and many businesses, restaurants and shops operate without it also), I was startled by how unaccustomed I was to that artificial cooling. For the first few days, I needed a sweatshirt or extra layer every time I stepped back indoors to feel comfortable.

Eventually I got used to the feel of AC again, and greatly appreciated it when the temperatures rose on the warm, humid days.

Larger Portion Sizes

I should write an entire post about how everything really is bigger in America. It was pretty jarring. The first example came when I was ordering dinner for my family in the Newark airport before catching our connecting flight to Indianapolis. I needed a jolt of caffeine to power through the last few hours of travel (especially with two kids to entertain), so I ordered a Diet Coke. The cashier asked me what size, and I requested a large without much thought. When she handed me what felt like a gallon of soda, I immediately realized I forgotten the meaning of "large" in the US.

Wide Highways

When my family drove out of the Indianapolis airport and hopped onto the interstate, I was truly awestruck by just how wide the highway that stretched before me was. Yes, there are large motorways here in the UK, but I rarely see 12 lanes of concrete with cars moving in either direction like I did that afternoon and it took me by surprise a bit.

Billboards

Maybe it's just the part of the UK where I live, but I rarely see billboards here. Immediately upon departing the airport, we were bombarded with them along the highway in Indiana.

Is American Football Popular Across the Pond?

For those who care about such things, the NFL football season officially kicked off this week. In the US, this is a big deal. According to most polls, it's America's most popular professional sport. But here in Great Britain? Understandably, not so much. Given that the NFL has undertaken a huge push to popularize the sport here across the pond, many friends back home have asked me if it's working. My short answer? Not from what I can tell.

In no particular order, here are a few observations about American football (not to be confused with football, known as soccer in the US)

- The NFL games in London look popular. Yes, that's true. The games have all been sold out. Regent Street gets decked out each week the NFL comes to town with banners and fanfare. But let me also say this: I know a handful of people who have attended the NFL games in London. They're all fellow American expats. I'm not saying the entire crowd is made up of Americans, but I also think a large number of them are.

- When we tell people we're from Indianapolis, if they are aware of the city at all, 75% of the time people identify it as the home of the Colts. This always really surprises me.

- One afternoon when I took my two boys to our village park, my son grabbed an American football for us to play with while there. He abandoned it for the swings and slide after a few minutes. Another boy, probably 10 years old, asked if he could play with it. He later told me he had never seen an American football in person before, and obviously had never played with one. Needless to say, I was the coolest mom at the park that day.

- Whenever we do have a conversation with people here about American football, they usually complain about all the breaks in between plays. They find that to be slow. I can definitely see why they feel that way. Since football/soccer and rugby are quite popular here, sports fans are more accustomed to fast moving games with little stoppage.

- The Super Bowl is televised here. It was on ITV4 last year. I tried to stay up and watch some of it last year. I didn't last long because it started so late, but I had to laugh at the commentators with their Scottish accents. It was hard to tell how much about American football they really understood. And without the commercials, it just wasn't the same!

- ITV4 also airs the Sunday Night game each week, but it's on at 1:30 a.m. so I never watch it. My family does subscribe to the NFL Game Pass, which cost about 100 pounds for us to watch all the games this year. We very rarely stream US television here, so we consider this is our one expat guilty pleasure. *(Go Colts!)*

In short, I think "football" fans here are far more interested in which team is leading in the Premier League than they are with the American version.

Noticeable Differences in Dining Out Between the US and UK

This week I was having a chat with a British friend who frequently travels to the US. She was asking me about our visit back to the States this summer, and we happened to get on the topic of dining out, restaurants, and food differences. As with many things, dining out in the UK can be quite different than dining out in the US. Here are a few general observations that we agreed on.

Expect a different level of attention from wait staff.

In the US, it is custom for your server to check in on you frequently throughout the meal. In the UK, this is not the case. In fact, you may have to call them over when you're ready to order and to pay the bill. The servers here are not being rude or inattentive. It's just a different way of doing it. In talking to many British people, they find US servers a bit overbearing at times during a meal. Like I said, it's just different expectations. And if think your drink is going to be refilled, forget it. If you want more, you'll need to order (and pay for) another.

It's typical here to eat in courses.

I realize this is true at finer restaurants in the US also, where you'd likely start with an appetizer or salad, and proceed from there. But even at somewhat casual places, like pubs, you're often served a first course (called a starter here), followed by your entrée (called a main) and finally dessert (called pudding).

Of course, this is entirely personal preference. You don't have to order a starter or pudding, but it is usually expected, especially at nicer restaurants.

The dining pace is slower.

For the reasons I mention above, you'll experience a slower pace when dining out here also. For me, this is a pro and a con. When I'm out at a restaurant with my young children, I'm sometimes annoyed that it can take quite a bit of time just to be served a simple meal, mostly because I have to entertain them during the long waits! But when I'm out on a date with my husband or out with friends, I appreciate that we aren't being rushed out the door to free up our table, like you sometimes experience in the US

It will cost more, comparatively.

Like with most things, expect to pay quite a bit more to dine out here also. This is true even at fast food restaurants. Looking for ways to save? You can grab a pretty cheap lunch by doing meal deals at grocery and convenience stores (usually a sandwich, crisps and a drink go for about £3). Pubs often have weeknight specials. My local has dining for two people for £15 on certain nights of the week. A restaurant in a nearby town has curry nights, where a curry dish and beer/wine go for about £8. They'll usually advertise these specials on signs and placards outside the restaurant door, so keep an eye out.

Tipping

The differences in tipping in the UK vs. the US is worthy of its own post, but I'll mention it briefly here.

You're only expected to tip about 10%, even if you really loved the service you received. For a cheap meal or just out to drinks, many people simply round up to the next whole pound. If you're paying with a credit card, you can ask your server to change the amount on the machine before they run your card and include your tip that way. Especially good to know if you don't have much cash or coins with you.

In short, I find people in the UK dine out more for pleasure, and not for convenience as is often the case in the US. I've had some of the best meals of my life here, but I've definitely paid a high price for that delicious food. Well worth the splurge occasionally, but not a regular part of our eating routine.

Going Native - British Things I Find Myself Saying

My husband and I recently attended a dinner party at someone's home, and it was set up as a murder mystery dinner. The characters we played were English, and so we spent the evening speaking in our best English accents among a bunch of English people (who speak with the genuine accent!). Needless to say, we do not have the accent mastered and everyone had some good laughs about our attempts.

But it did get me thinking about what British sayings I have incorporated into my speech over the last 16 months. Here are a few:

"Sort it out"

I find myself saying various forms of "we'll sort that out" or "let's get it sorted" or "that will sort itself out." In place of "we'll figure that out" or "let's figure it out."

"Tuck in" to food

This started as a joke between my husband and I. We often hear people say, mostly in food advertisements, to "tuck into" their delicious food, meaning to start eating. So before meals, we'd tell the kids to "tuck in" and be overly dramatic about it. And now it has stuck, and we actually say it in all seriousness.

"Come round to ours"

People tend to use this expression when encouraging someone to stop by or pay them a visit. I now find myself saying this when making plans or texting with friends. It sounded a bit strange to me at first, and now I think it's really charming and welcoming.

"Put the kettle on"

I've always been a tea drinker, even before moving to England. But instead of saying "I'll boil some water" or "let me make some tea," I now say the much more British sounding "put the kettle on." It's particularly true here in this country, where most people use an electric kettle, and so you really are switching something on!

"Be sensible"

Within the first few days of my son starting school, he mentioned to me that he had been a very sensible boy that day. Sensible is definitely not a word he had ever used before, so I knew he had picked it up at school. As he describes it, you can either act sensible or silly. And so I now try to encourage my boys to be sensible. I love this way of describing, in a simple way, appropriate behavior to young children.

"xx"

I mentioned this in another post, but many people here will sign a quick note, text, email, or comment on social media with a "x" or "xx." Now that I better understand it, I think it's a sweet way of showing a bit of affection without overdoing it.

These expressions are obviously in addition to the many items in everyday life that have a different word here (like pants vs. trousers, diapers vs. nappies, etc.) I try to use these as much as possible, mostly to avoid confusion and strange looks!

More Things I've Had to Google Since Moving to the UK

As I've now lived here for 18 months, you would think I'd have most things figured out...but I still learn something new almost every day! So here's a new installment of Things I've Had to Google.

When do we change the clocks?

I guess I thought the weekend you change the clocks (backward in the fall, forward in the spring) was somewhat universal around the globe. Nope. Sure enough, this fall the UK is changing a week prior to the US. Which I actually love, as it means for at least one week, my family is only 4 hours different from me.

Where did Prince Harry go to university?

You hear a lot about how the Duke and Duchess of Cambridge met at university (St. Andrews in Scotland). So I started to wonder where Prince Harry went. Turns out, there's a reason you don't hear much about Prince Harry's university career. After taking a gap year following his time at Eton, he went straight into the military.

What do children wear to discos?

During my son's first year of school, there was a disco held one afternoon after school hours. As an American, when I think of disco, I think of John Travolta and the music of the 1970s.

I had a feeling, though, that I shouldn't dress my 4-year-old up in polyester bell bottom trousers. Fortunately, I quickly learned that a disco is just another name for a dance. (And after consulting with some other parents at school, he wore jeans and a nice shirt and fit right in!)

What is bric-a-brac?

One evening, my doorbell rang and a nice woman was standing there with a large bag and asked me if I had any bric-a-brac for the village fete. I was polite, but terribly confused, so I just said I didn't. Later I jumped on the computer to see what she was looking for. Bric-a-brac is just a term for things you might want to sell, like household goods or antiques. This sale was part of a fundraiser for our village.

Was Boris Johnson born in the US?

Some Americans may remember London's mayor from the 2012 Summer Olympics or other moments when London has been in the news. He's quite a character. One evening we were watching an interview with him, and my husband mentioned that he heard a rumor that Johnson has aspirations to be the first person to be British Prime Minister *and* US President. After an internet search, it appears he was in fact born in the US, so in theory, this political progression is possible. I have no idea if he truly aspires to that, however.

What day is Thanksgiving?

I'm a little embarrassed to share that as I was working on plans for my family and a few other expat families to celebrate, I had to turn to the internet to figure out what day Thanksgiving is.

None of my calendars, all purchased here in the UK, had it listed and I couldn't figure out if it was Thursday, November 27 or the week prior.

So there's a little peek into my Google search history. Just one of the many ways being an American in the UK is a constant learning opportunity.

How I Eat Differently Since Moving Abroad

I roasted a chicken this weekend, something I often do since moving to the UK, and it occurred to me that it might be fitting to discuss some of the ways my eating habits have changed since moving here. I should note that these are simply my experiences. I think eating habits vary drastically, both across cultures and within them. I don't intend to speak for all Americans who move to the UK (or certainly not all Americans in general), and I definitely don't think my eating habits reflect the British population as a whole. It's simply a reflection of how my family and I have eaten differently since relocating across the pond.

More varieties of fruits and vegetables

I've always been a moderately healthy eater. I indulge in lots of temptations, of course, but overall, I've eaten a fairly balanced diet since I was a kid. A few months after moving to the UK, I signed up for a produce box delivery from an organic food company. Each Monday, a box full of 3 kinds of fruits and 4 types of vegetables shows up at my door. I love the convenience of the delivery, (It often allows me to delay a trip to the grocery store!), but most importantly, it has forced me to learn to cook types of produce I wouldn't normally. We now regularly eat leeks, kale, pomegranates, chard, parsnips, etc. Even when they don't get delivered in my box, I find that I often buy them now. I subscribed to a similar service in the US, but it was only in the summer months and the types of produce were much more familiar to me.

Cooking at home more often

Typically, we go out to lunch on Saturday or Sunday, and that is our only meal out of the house each week. We probably ate out at least 2-3 times per week when living in the US. In part this is due to the cost, as it's more expensive to eat out here. But we also live near far fewer family-friendly restaurants than we did in the US, and since we have young children, this also limits our restaurant habits. It's been a positive change for the most part, but I definitely miss it at times (since I'm typically the one who cooks).

More simple, cooked-from-scratch meals

Because I cook much more often now, I've simplified what I make. No more casseroles with 7 steps and 20 ingredients. I'm much more likely to roast a chicken along with potatoes and carrots. An hour in the oven and I have a healthy, filling meal for my family. (Plus, a small chicken is cheaper than buying a package of chicken breasts, typically!) I then use the chicken bones to make my own broth to use in soups later in the week or to freeze (again, something I wouldn't have done previously). We eat a lot more sausage and various cheeses also. We no longer rely on boxes or mixes, since those aren't quite as common here either (or at least not the kinds or brands we were accustomed to eating). That's probably been the biggest, healthiest change we've made.

Greater reliance on store-made meals

These are called ready-meals here. I rarely cooked frozen or already prepared meals in the US. A frozen lasagna from Stouffers didn't really appeal to me.

But the ready-meals here (especially those from the nicer grocery stores) are of rather good quality and relatively healthy and affordable. And they're usually not frozen but freshly made.

British recipes, but not British dishes

I learned within the first few months of living here that cooking with American recipes was a pain. Converting quantities and cooking temperature, even just finding the right ingredients was sometimes impossible. If I'm making a new recipe, it's almost always from a British source so that I don't have to bother with any of that. But I also found that I rarely make typical British dishes like fish pie, bangers and mash, etc. I much prefer to eat these dishes when I dine out (or as ready-meals) instead.

Making Mexican food at home more often

I've mentioned a few times in this column that I really miss decent Mexican food. What I've had here, with the exception of a couple of restaurants in London, has been pretty awful. (Understandably so— we're quite a ways away from Mexico!) But my whole family loves this type of food, so I make a Mexican-style meal at least every few weeks now. This was something I rarely did in the US, only because it was easier to just dine out for that type of cuisine (and sometimes cheaper, too).

When I dine out, I splurge.

I tend to not make very healthy choices when we do go out to eat. I used to order entrée-sized salads quite often in the US. Now I'm more likely to get fish 'n' chips.

I'm not sure why this is; maybe because we don't eat out as often, so I'm inclined to not watch what I eat very carefully when I do. Maybe there are fewer healthy options on a typical British menu that appeal to me as I might find in the US. Regardless, I try not to worry about this too much since we often eat fairly healthy at home.

But let's not discuss my Cadbury chocolate habit. A gal should never reveal all her secrets, right?

An American's Take on the Most Popular British Chocolate Bars

Like most of you, I've been reading with great interest about the recent decision to ban many British chocolate bars from being sold in the US. Fortunately, for now, I'm able to get my hands on these delightful treats without any trouble. I'm a huge lover of the chocolate here. It's creamy, not at all bitter, but also not too sweet. Delicious! I plan on filling a huge container with my favorites to send with all my belongings when we move back. (Ban or no ban!)

I thought it would be interesting to take a look at the 10 most popular chocolate bars here in the UK (as determined by IRI Worldwide, based on value sales).

10) M&M'S: One of two American products to appear on the list. I was surprised to see them on the list as they don't strike me as being popular here. Instead, I often see Smarties. (In the UK, Smarties are small chocolate discs similar to M&M'S, not like the little sour discs called Smarties in the US.) You won't find all the crazy varieties of M&M'S here in the UK as you do in the US. I typically only see the plain and peanut here.

9) Wispa: This was a new one to me. I had seen Wispa in stores but hadn't tried it myself until now. I thought it was quite good. It tastes very similar to a regular Cadbury Dairy Milk (more on that to come), but with a much lighter texture.

8) Nestle Aero: This is similar to the Wispa in the sense that it has a lighter texture. But the Aero achieves this through small air pockets that look like little circles when you bite into it. I definitely prefer the Cadbury taste over Nestle, but it was still tasty.

7) Twirl. Another bar produced by Cadbury. Twirl is structured almost like thin chocolate ribbons all compacted together. It also has a lighter texture compared to a standard, solid bar of chocolate. It seems very similar to the Cadbury Flake, which is a very common addition to an ice cream cone here. Sure enough, when I read up on the Twirl, it uses the same technology in production as the Flake.

6) Snickers. It's the other American chocolate bar to make it onto this list. I noticed it was also the only chocolate bar containing nuts to make the list.

5) Mars. An American reading this might assume the Mars bar is something different, as there is a chocolate bar in America called Mars, too. But the UK Mars bar is much more similar to the American Milky Way bar. It's got nougat with a thin layer of caramel. (Seriously, chocolate makers, can we start coming up with some new names for things so as to avoid international confusion!?)

4) Maltesers. Just like M&M'S, these don't usually come in "bar" form, but are instead small balls (insert your favorite Tom Brady joke here). They taste similar to a malt ball. If you like your chocolate treat with a lot of crunch, these are for you.

3) Kit Kat. If you're an American like me, you might have assumed these are an American product. But they're not! Kit Kats were originally made by a chocolate company in York, England. They sold the rights to Kit Kat in the US to Hershey's, and then later sold the rights in the UK to Nestle. So apparently there's a slight difference between a US Kit Kat and a UK Kit Kat. I haven't had an American one in so long I can't tell you what that would be, though. (And I suspect the British one is better.)

2) Galaxy. This is a standard, solid chocolate bar. Very delicious. But I don't find Galaxy bars to be as creamy as Cadbury Dairy Milk, which are my favorite. I think the Cadbury/Galaxy showdown is just about personal preference. I happen to love my chocolate super creamy.

1) Cadbury Dairy Milk. I was pleased to see these topped the list, as they are my favorite too. I can't help but wonder if my own purchases of these bars since moving here pushed them to the top of the list (kidding—kind of)! As I said, I love how creamy they are. In fact, Cadbury boasts that there's a "glass and a half of milk in every bar." I'm sure that's just a marketing ploy, but it works!

Things That Might Surprise You About British Television

I've mentioned a few times that I don't watch much television (aside from children's programs and shows I get hooked on from Netflix). Therefore, I don't often write about British television here Anglotopia. (Fortunately there's plenty of info about that on the site from others!) But anyone who has lived in the UK as long as I have will notice a few things about television here that might surprise some Americans, particularly if you've never had the chance to visit and watch it for yourself.

There are many current American shows on here. I suppose it isn't really that shocking that a lot of American television shows would be on in the UK. After all, the American entertainment industry does seem to dominate around the world. But I think what surprised me most about this is that it's not just old episodes of dated shows (like *Everybody Loves Raymond* or *Frazier*, although you'll find both on here). But you'll also find current (and popular) shows like *The Big Bang Theory*, *Homeland*, *The Good Wife* and others. And typically, only a season (or sometimes just a few episodes) behind what's on in the US.

This includes American reality television shows. Unfortunately, it's not just some of the better quality programs that make their way across the pond. The *Kardashians*, all of *The Real Housewives* series, *Teen Mom*, *Storage Wars*, and many more often fill my television channels, especially during the day.

I hate to think British people learn about what Americans might be like in real life from these shows. I'm sure they have enough sense to know most of the people on those shows are not the norm.

There are many British reality shows, too! I think this may surprise me the most of all. If you think trashy reality program is just an American phenomenon, you're wrong. Perhaps the US invented it, but it's been embraced here, too (though not by all, I'm sure). There are UK equivalents to many of the US shows, like *I'm A Celebrity Get Me Out of Here*, *Big Brother*, *The Apprentice* and more. But they also have their own spin on the reality sector. *Geordie Shore* seems similar to MTV's *Jersey Shore*. There are countless dating and matchmaking shows. *Come Dine with Me* is a funny dining/cooking show. I could go on and on. Luckily, they're not all trashy. A show I happen to really enjoy is called *24 Hours in A&E*, where the cameras spend a full day in an emergency room department in a hospital, and chronicle the stories of some of the patients that are seen. I find it fascinating.

Very little local news programming. The only local news I see on television are brief snippets during the national news programming in the morning and evening.

No Commercials. There are no commercials on any of the BBC stations. I love this!

Popular Shows on the Weekends. Many of the more popular shows air on Saturday and Sunday evening. In the US, you'd never air popular programming on a Saturday night. Yet *Strictly Come Dancing*, *X Factor*, *Downton Abbey*, *Call the Midwife*, and *Britain's Got Talent*, all air on Saturday or Sunday nights and are considered some of the most popular shows here.

Soap Operas. Soap operas are on in the evening. While weekday afternoons are prime soap opera time in the US, here the popular soaps air during the early evening hours. Favorite like *EastEnders* and *Coronation Stree*t are on most days around 7 or 8 p.m.

The Tale of Two Royal Births

One of the first big news events that took place after we moved here two summers ago was the birth of Prince George to the Duke and Duchess of Cambridge. It was fun to experience such an important occasion to the country we were now calling home for a few years. Like many Americans, I find myself a bit fascinated with the royal family and it's hard to deny the charm of Prince William and Princess Catherine's growing family. So it was fun to do it all over again with the birth of Princess Charlotte earlier this month. I thought I'd offer a little insight into what it's like to live here during these moments and compare/contrast the two births.

UK media covers these events differently than the US media does. I remember a friend telling me that all the American morning news programs had reporters stationed at the hospital where Prince George was to be born weeks in advance of his arrival. I was shocked, as I hadn't heard much about the impending due date from the British media that I watch regularly. In fact, when the expected arrival was covered at all by the British media during the lead-up, it was mostly focused on how many members of the foreign press had gathered, and not about the birth itself.

That being said, once Prince George and Princess Charlotte were born, it was certainly given quite a bit of attention by the news outlets here. When I heard (via text from family in America, ironically enough) that the Duchess had gone into labor with Princess Charlotte, I turned on the BBC and they covered it almost exclusively that entire afternoon and evening.

But for the most part, life went on as usual immediately following both births. I didn't hear many people discussing it. You won't find people honking horns or celebrating in the streets. In fact, if you didn't pay much attention to the news, you probably wouldn't realize what was going on at all.

One thing I really respect about the way these events are handled here is that both the press and the general public seem to respect the privacy of the family. Yes, we're all curious to hear about names and details and even what they wear as they leave the hospital, but there is a general understanding that one should just patiently wait for those things to be announced via the formal channels instead of prying by any means necessary. And once the family has headed home, you don't hear much about comings and goings other than bits and pieces about which relatives visited when. To be honest, I typically read up on the royal family via American news outlets.

So how did the news of Princess Charlotte's birth compare to Prince George's? A few differences:

The lead-up was much more low-key this time around. Or, at least, that was my impression. I certainly didn't hear about hundreds, if not thousands, of press gathered for weeks outside the hospital like I heard about with Prince George.

The aftermath was also much more subdued. As the BBC reported live from Buckingham Palace following the placement of the sign that formally announced her birth, there were certainly crowds gathered to see it. But it almost looked like any other busy Saturday at a major tourist attraction in central London. Whereas when Prince George was born, there was a huge sea of humanity outside the gates for hours.

It began and ended much more quickly with Princess Charlotte. This is due in large part to the fact that the Duchess's labor was far shorter, and they entered and departed the hospital all within the same day. The press simply didn't have two straight days to obsess over who would visit and when. I think because the public also knew what to expect (as in, there would be photos with the couple and the new princess, then they would depart the hospital, then her name would be announced, then they'd likely leave London for a period of time), it seemed much more straight forward.

Some things that were the same? There was still all the pomp and circumstance (like gun salutes). And stores still scrambled to sell keepsakes and souvenirs once the gender and name were revealed. (And I still bought a copy of a newspaper to keep as a souvenir... you'll see the two side by side in the photo above.)

I like to think that someday when Prince George becomes king, I'll tell my grandchildren about how I lived in the UK during his birth!

A Guide to British Charity Days

I was scrolling through Facebook a few days ago when something about Red Nose Day popped up. It made me pause, because Red Nose Day was a couple of months ago. And then I realized it was from an American source (I honestly can't remember which one). Since when did Americans participate in Red Nose Day? I certainly had never heard of it until I moved here.

For those of you in the dark about Red Nose Day and other such prominent charity days here in the UK, I thought I'd write a little bit about them. It was certainly something I spent some time "figuring out" the first year I lived here.

First of all, these are days (or sometimes a full week) when the whole country rallies behind and raises money for a particular charity. It can be in the form of a simple coffee morning or cake stall (like a bake sale) where money is raised for the cause. Or perhaps you dress in fancy dress (costumes). Often there is a telethon held on the television on the Friday evening where you can call or text donations. On these, there will be live music, comedians, lots of celebrities, etc., similar to the Stand Up to Cancer program in America that is shown on television once a year.

What always strikes me is how all-encompassing it is. My son's school participates in these. My husband's office does. I once met a friend for coffee at my village pub on one of these days, and the money we spent on coffee and a slice of cake was all donated to the charity.

The grocery stores all sell special merchandise and products related to the cause (and donate proceeds to the charity). Sometimes there's even a special song released by a famous artist in support of the day. Unless you never left your house and never turned on your television, it would be difficult to ignore these special days.

So what are these days? I haven't kept an exact record, but off the top of my head, here are a few of the major ones:

Macmillan Cancer

This is normally just one day in September. You'll see Macmillan's trademark color, green, everywhere, including lots and lots of balloons outside shops, restaurants, and gatherings. This day is mostly celebrated with coffee mornings, where groups gather for a "cuppa" and some cake and everyone donates money for cancer research and support. In fact, they call it the World's Biggest Coffee Morning. Macmillan is an organization that provides support to cancer patients and their families.

Children in Need

This is celebrated for several days in November. Children in Need is a charity of the BBC that then provides grants to many organizations around the UK that assist children who need assistance. For the past two years, my oldest son could wear pajamas to school one day as long as we donated a pound. My youngest son's nursery had the kids dress in various themes all week for a small donation.

You'll hear it mentioned constantly by radio and television presenters (on the BBC, naturally) and there's a huge telethon at the end of the week. The symbol of Children in Need is Pudsey, and lots of Pudsey products are available at the shops.

Red Nose Day

This is the event that apparently has crossed the pond into America this year. Red Nose Day is typically held in March here in the UK. It's a charity day that supports Comic Relief, which gives grants to organizations around the world and in the UK to alleviate poverty. It also has a telethon. My sons were allowed to wear whacky clothes to school that day, including colorful socks and neckties. The symbol of the event is a clown's red nose, and you could buy red noses and other affiliated products all over town. I even saw lots of red noses on the front of many people's cars.

Sports Relief

Sports Relief supports Comic Relief (mentioned above, also affiliated with Red Nose Day). There's another television program to raise money for this event, also, typically held in March. My son's school did a big sports competition that day, and I found myself buying Sports Relief wristbands for him to wear.

World Book Day

This is one of my favorites because children in schools across the country dress up as their favorite book character, which I think is such a great idea. My son went as Beatrix Potter's Peter Rabbit this year and it was adorable.

It's less about fundraising and more about each child who participates getting a token for a £1 book. This was celebrated in March in the UK, but is typically held in April in other parts of the world.

I'm sure I've missed other important charity days, but these were the big ones I could remember. I've really enjoyed participating in them and they seem to raise so much money.

My Favorite Antique Finds
Living in England

One of the things I've had a chance to do over the past year is attending a few different antique fairs or festivals held in my area of England. I am definitely a novice when it comes to this sort of thing, and going to an antique market would probably not rank high on my list of leisure time activities if I were back in the US (not that there's anything wrong with it whatsoever, I'm just not a big shopper of any kind). But it has turned out to be a really fascinating insight into history and culture here. A few of my favorite "souvenirs" that I've picked up while at these events:

Trench Art

A friend of mine who had moved to the UK from Belgium introduced me to trench art. They are shell casings that soldiers sculpted into works of art while spending time in the trenches (mostly during World War I). My artwork is a casing that has been turned into a vase, date stamped 1908, and was produced by a British military supplier (all things I could glean via Google based on what's stamped on the casing). I bought it for £18 (approximately $25). I absolutely love it, particularly because commemorating major anniversaries of these two wars have been important milestones during our time living here.

A Street Sign

I have grand ideas of creating a wall of photos and other mementos from our time living abroad in whatever house we live in back in the US.

I want a constant reminder of this phase of our lives. So I was thrilled to find an old "children crossing" sign. I've spent the past two years shepherding two small children around the UK and continental Europe and the symbolism of this sign means a lot to me. I bought this for £10 (approximately $15).

Peter Rabbit China Set

My children became really interested in Peter Rabbit, a children's character from books by Beatrix Potter, during our visit to the Lake District, where Potter lived most of her life. I'm very interested in finding each of my sons a few keepsakes that will help them to remember that they spent part of their childhood living in the UK, and I think this set will be something they can pass down to their children. I can't remember what I paid for this, but it was less than £20, and consists of a plate, small bowl, and small tea cup, all with illustrations and quotes from the books. I'm hoping at future antique shopping trips I can find a Paddington Bear collectible that I like, as he's another favorite of my boys.

An Official Handbook of My Town

I was at an antique festival about an hour's drive from where I live a few months ago. I was digging through a box of old books and suddenly I saw an old drawing that I immediately recognized. It was the same view I see as I drive into town each day. Turns out, it was a handbook from the town, dated 1936. It's so fascinating to see how life has changed, and yet what has remained the same. The best part was that I bought it for £3 (about 5 bucks)!

I'm very thankful that some of my more shopping-savvy friends have invited me along on these antique adventures because I will cherish not only the items I purchased, but also the memories of the fun we've had hunting for these gems.

What I'm Excited to Eat in the US as I Visit Home

I'll be back in the US for a couple of weeks in August. This is our second visit back to our home state of Indiana since we moved to England more than two years ago. While I'm mostly just excited to see family and friends that we haven't seen in months or years, I've also got a list of food and drink I can't wait to indulge in while there.

I'm a little embarrassed to share this list, as it is extremely unhealthy, but I'm guessing any expat can relate. After all, it's not the fruit and vegetables that you miss (since you can likely get those wherever you are)! Please know that on a normal day I eat relatively healthy, exercise regularly, and rarely eat out. So I don't feel too guilty about indulging in some of these temptations while I'm in the US next month.

Mexican Food

I'm sure I've mentioned a few times (or maybe a few dozen) that I miss good Mexican food. We've found a couple of places in London that do great Mexican, but nothing near our house. I can't wait to indulge in a margarita, chips and restaurant-style salsa, and queso. I bet I'll eat Mexican 3 or 4 times during my two-week stay. (I hope so, anyway!)

Gray Brothers Cafeteria

Most of you readers will have never heard of this, but it's a cafeteria-style restaurant in the southwest suburbs of Indianapolis.

I haven't been in years, but for some reason, I'm craving their fried chicken, macaroni and cheese, and strawberry pie. Very classic American food here!

Yats: Another local restaurant with locations around Indianapolis, this place serves up the most amazing Cajun/Creole food. Needless to say, you don't find Cajun food in rural England!

A Few Fast Food Places: I can get some American fast food here in England (McDonald's, KFC, Burger King, and Subway are pretty common). But I'd love to go to Panera Bread for lunch during my visit, maybe get a Frosty from Wendy's, a chalupa from Taco Bell, a Dairy Queen Reese's Cup Blizzard, and just a few weeks ago I strangely started missing Cracker Barrel. I'm sure I won't get to all these places, but they all sound delicious after a year away!

Iced Tea: Is it weird to miss tea while living in England? I do miss drinking iced tea in the summer. You can buy it here (like sweetened Lipton varieties in various flavors), and sometimes I make it myself at home. But just this weekend, I was sitting outside on the patio of my local pub on a sunny day, and a big glass of iced tea would have been fantastic.

My Family's Cooking: I can't wait to eat my mom's potato salad, my dad's barbecued ribs, homegrown tomatoes from various relative's gardens, etc. I can (and have) made some of my mom's specialties since we moved here, but as I often tell her, it tastes better when she makes it.

Frozen Yogurt by the Weight: I'm sure most Americans are familiar with the many frozen yogurt places that allow you to add your own toppings and just pay for your treat by the weight. I love these places and miss taking my kids there.

Again, please don't judge my eating habits based on this post. In fact, I had a salad for dinner tonight

Moments of Reverse Culture Shock Returning to the USA

Last fall, after I returned from a three-week trip back to the US to visit friends and family. This year, I'm back from a two-week trip, but had even more moments of culture shock being back in America after essentially two years away.

4-Way Stop Signs

I switch between driving on the right and left fairly easily (we've driven enough on holidays in Europe to have become accustomed to that change). But each time I approached a 4-way stop sign in the US, I had a brief moment of confusion, especially if other cars pulled up at the same time. This type of intersection is so rare where I live in England and I had forgotten the basic etiquette. I'm a pro at roundabouts now!

Eating Times

One of my pet peeves living in the UK is that restaurants either don't open or don't start serving lunch until noon at the earliest. Yet while I was back in the US this summer, I couldn't believe how busy some restaurants were by 11:30 a.m., sometimes even 11 a.m. I tend to eat early, both lunch and dinner, so I have to say I was pretty happy with this cultural shift.

Abundance of Stores

Maybe it's that I live in a fairly rural area of England, compared with the busy suburban area of Indiana where I spent time this summer.

But I could not get over how many stores and shopping areas there were while I was in the US. It seemed pretty extreme to have a giant Walmart, right next to a Super Target, right next to a Meijer. Or two large drugstores directly across the street. It just struck me as excessive. (Although I sometimes complain that it takes me 20 minutes to drive to a grocery story here where I live in England, so I guess I can't have it both ways!)

Toilets

This observation makes me chuckle every time I think of it. Last summer, my youngest son (2 at the time, now 3) was still in diapers. Now he's potty trained, and this was the first time he ever used an American toilet. He couldn't believe how much water was inside them, and he was completely panicked it was going to overflow each time he used the toilet for the first few days.

Garages and Basements

My older son (age 6) kept asking me questions about everyone's garages. It's pretty rare to see a 2-bay garage, much less a 3-bay garage in England, and rarely do people park a car in their garage here. Most garages here are detached from houses, so he thought it was so cool to walk right into someone's house from the garage while we were in the US.

He also noticed most of our friends and family had basements. It actually led to a pretty interesting conversation about tornadoes (and why basements are sometimes a necessity in parts of America).

American Flags

Both my kids spent the bulk of the time we were in the car getting to various places counting all the American flags they saw. I never paid attention to how many homes and business fly the flag until this visit. So when I returned to England this week, I paid close attention to this. There are only two houses in my village that fly a flag (one flies the English flag, the other the British flag). The pub in my village also flies a flag. Otherwise, we don't see many unless we're at large gatherings or big attractions. I am a huge fan of flags of all kinds, so I find this difference so fascinating. (In our house, we have a small British flag and a small American flag in our playroom.)

My Tea Drinking Habits

One of the things you realize pretty early on when moving to England from the US is that the reputation this country has as being a bit tea fanatical is well-deserved. Indeed, it permeates everyday life here. I thought I'd share a few funny stories, observations, and how my own tea drinking habits have changed since I moved here 2 ½ years ago.

First, a little about my personal tea drinking habits. Before moving to England, I did drink hot tea occasionally. Whenever I was sick, on really cold days, or if I was just craving something warm to drink. Sometimes I would have a cup when spending time with my mom or my mother-in-law, since they both drink it as well. But that was about it.

Since moving here, I have a cup almost daily. If I meet friends out for "coffee," it's actually tea that most of us typically order. If I visit friends at their house, that's usually what we drink. I almost always make a cup of tea when I get home in the late afternoon. (I usually spend an hour outdoors watching my kids play outside at the school playground in the afternoon, so I often crave a cup of tea to warm me back up once we get home.)

But on warm summer days, I don't drink hot tea. That part of me remains firmly "American," I suppose, because all the British people I know drink tea regardless of the weather.

This summer, I was once on a train back home from London. It was late afternoon and the train had been parked at King's Cross for about 30 minutes before it departed. Needless to say, the carriage I was in had grown quite warm (they're rarely air conditioned). Yet the group of women sitting across the aisle from me was complaining that it had been at least 10 minutes and the tea cart hadn't been by. They each had a cold bottle of water with them, yet it was hot tea they wanted to drink! I couldn't believe it.

I still do drink iced tea. I know most Brits cannot understand this drink and don't enjoy it, but I love to drink it in the summer. I make it myself since I don't often find it at restaurants and the bottles sold in stores are usually already sweetened, which I don't really enjoy. In fact, saying "hot tea" when ordering at a restaurant will instantly mark you as a tourist. You can simply say tea; the hot is assumed.

It's also still not my caffeine-fix of choice. Like many people, I need a jolt of caffeine to keep me going throughout the day, but I almost always turn to coffee first thing in the morning (and maybe Diet Coke around lunch time) for that. If I make tea at home, it's usually caffeine-free, actually. I was recently at a driver training course, and we were in a small room adjacent to a government building. When the instructor told the group that there was no kettle in the room and that they'd have to go without tea or coffee until after the 4-hour course was over, there was nearly a revolt among my fellow students.

All that said, I have developed a few British-like traits when it comes to tea:

I have a particular way of making it. Boil fresh water in the kettle. Pour over my tea bag. Let it sit for a few minutes. Then add a bit of milk. I have to admit that I used to just splash the hot water and milk and tea bag all in at the same time. (There is a debate among people here about milk first or after, but I prefer to let the tea brew in the water before adding milk.)

I rarely drink it "to go." In America it is so commonplace to see people walking around or driving in their car with a to-go mug or cup. Here, sitting down to a cup of tea is just that: sitting down. I like that is has a strong connection between stopping what you're doing and taking a moment to rest with your cup of tea.

I can no longer tolerate tea out of a paper or Styrofoam cup. It just tastes awful. Yet I often drank it this way in the US. I must have a proper mug now.

I now know to offer tea to every person that comes to my door. My apologies to the first few maintenance people that came to my home when we first moved here and I only offered water. I now realize what a horrible faux pas I was making!

I'm addicted to my electric kettle. Someone told me they sell these in the US now. (Maybe they did when I lived there, but I just never realized it!) I'll definitely be buying one when we move back. Boiling water in seconds—you can't beat that!

The Keurig craze hasn't quite taken off here. Yes, the machines exist here, but they just aren't nearly as prevalent in people's homes as in the US. I had one before we moved, but I doubt I'll use one when we move back.

I also love to have a sweet treat with a cup of tea now. In December, I often treat myself to a big cup of tea and a small mince pie in the evenings after I've put my kids to bed. I also love tea with a biscuit (cookie). I never did this before we moved here.

And don't forget, the word tea can also refer to food. Afternoon tea is a full production of cakes, scones and little sandwiches. And an early dinner or family meal in the evening is called tea, also. It's usually obvious what people mean by "tea" based on the context of the sentence, but every once in a while I get confused still.

My Favorite British Radio Stories

One of the things I miss about my life back in the US was my favorite radio station. (A shout out to 92.3 WTTS in Indianapolis!) It played the perfect combination of my favorite musical styles and genres and I even liked the DJs. I haven't found anything similar to it here where I live in the UK, so it's always been something that makes me a little homesick.

But that's not to say I don't enjoy listening to the radio here. In fact, I often find myself laughing out loud in the car because of something I've heard. One thing to note is that I live in a somewhat rural part of the country. I'm really only able to get about 6 radio stations to come in clearly as I drive around. So I may not have the same experiences you have had listening to the radio here in part due to that.

I love the lack of commercials. Like the BBC television stations, the BBC radio stations don't air commercials (or advertisements). That's not to say it's constant music or programming, since they do spend a lot of time plugging their own events and things, but it still makes listening, especially over long periods of time, much more pleasant. Other radio stations do air advertising regularly, similar to what you experience on US radio.

The frequencies for the BBC radio stations don't seem to change as you drive around. I can drive from my house down to the tip of Cornwall (6 hours away!) and if I'm listening to a BBC station, I never have to fuss with the dial. Isn't that great?

One of the stations I listen to regularly, a HEART radio station based out of Cambridge, airs what they call "Big Town Showdown," a ten-question quiz show where callers participate as representatives of their town or village. I love shouting out the answers and I especially love when they have a question about America, as the contestants often get it wrong. ("What's the ocean found on the west coast of the US?" and "How many letters are in the US state of Utah?" are two of my favorites that people missed. And I'm not judging; I'm just as pathetic when it comes to questions that are specific to the UK sometimes!)

Heart also does a "school run" afternoon radio program, which airs during the time I'm driving to pick my kids up from school (Obviously!). Parents and kids call in and share accomplishments or request songs and I get a kick out of it.

The radio station located closest to me is called Rutland Radio. It's very local, and one of the things that always makes me laugh is when they read out descriptions of lost pets to see if anyone has seen "the lost tabby in Cottesmore" or whatever the case may be. (The idea of a pet being lost isn't what makes me laugh, it's just that I would never dream of hearing that on air in the US.)

I also once heard a traffic report on that station describing the potential for a backup at a temporary light in a nearby village. The village happened to be mine, and I could actually see the temporary traffic light directly from my kitchen window. I was tempted to call in and let them know there wasn't a single car waiting at the light so they could probably take that off their traffic update.

And my favorite British radio moment is when the BBC airs the national traffic report. To think that in the span of a few minutes you can cover traffic for an entire country reminds me that this is still just a relatively small island. Sometimes in day-to-day living, it doesn't seem like that.

Attending a British Children's Birthday Party

I've written several posts pertaining to how raising children is different in Britain. In many ways, this is the aspect of day-to-day living we know the most about since we moved here with an 18-month-old and a 4-year-old (who are now almost 4 and 6 ½). In this age range, birthday parties often fill our weekends and we've observed a lot of cultural differences in this regard.

Often the children wear costumes (or fancy dress, as they say here). Pirates or super heroes and princesses are the most popular choices. As my oldest son has gotten older, this tradition seems to be going away, but now my youngest is entering into the fancy dress party stage of childhood here.

In the US I had typically only been to children's parties with a handful of friends, maybe a dozen kids at the most. Here, it has been customary to invite the entire class of children, so some of the parties we have attended have 30 or more children. For this reason, probably, the parties are rarely held at children's homes and almost always at a rented village hall or party venue, like a large soft play center (soft play places are sort of like an indoor playground, most towns here have at least one and they do make great locations for children's parties).

Most of the parties we've attended have had a hired children's entertainer who have led the kids in a series of games or dances or other activities. Some have had a theme, like an entertainer dressed as Cinderella, a science-based party where the kids did crazy experiments, etc. Others were almost more like a DJ where they played fun music and got the kids running around and dancing. Popular games here are Pass the Parcel and Musical Statues.

The children are usually served a light meal, like cheese and jam sandwiches, crisps (chips), maybe some fruit and vegetables, too, and a small sweet for pudding (dessert). The adults are always offered tea or coffee and maybe a biscuit, but don't usually eat a meal like the children do.

One of the strangest differences comes with the birthday cake. At parties here, you still light candles and sing happy birthday, but they then slice the cake up, wrap it in a napkin, and stick the cake in the party bag to be sent home with the child. I still don't understand why the children don't eat the cake at the party, instead of eating it once it's been all smashed up in a napkin when we get home.

But one tradition I love is that the birthday girl or boy doesn't open presents at the party. You simply bring a small gift, leave it in a pile of presents, and that's the last of it. Then there's no awkward moment if someone gets the same thing twice, etc., and no one feels like they need to bring the best gift. Thank you notes are definitely the custom here too and we usually get one within a week or two of the party.

I must admit that I haven't thrown a large party for either of my kids while we've lived here, as I've found it a little overwhelming. And we were accustomed to celebrating birthdays with just our families anyway when we were in the US. But my kids have certainly had fun celebrating with their friends and classmates over the past few years.

Do My Children Have English Accents?

The question I'm asked most often, by friends, family, people I barely know, people in America and people here in the UK, is: do my children have English accents yet? And if so, when did they start sounding English? It's one of the aspects of being an American expat here in the UK with young children that I have found so fascinating to see develop over the past 2 ½ years.

First, I've already written about the fact that my kids (and quite honestly, now my husband and I) use a lot of English terminology or phrases. That started pretty early on in our expat experience. But do my boys (my youngest turns 4 in a few weeks and my oldest is 6 ½) have an accent? The answer is yes, and kind of. I'll explain further.

The most interesting thing to me is that my children have developed accents in different ways and at different levels. When we moved here, I would have guessed that my oldest would develop a full accent, given that he was in an English school all day. I assumed my youngest would only have a slight accent, given that he would still mostly be at home with me. What actually has happened is the complete opposite. I'll explain how both kids have progressed.

My Youngest: When we moved to England, my youngest was 18 months old. He wasn't speaking very much. So he has basically learned to talk here in the UK. I would describe his accent as nearly fully English.

In fact, as he learned to talk, like most moms I sometimes had trouble understanding him. But there were times when this happened because I didn't realize he was actually speaking with an accent. The story that best illustrates this is one day, as we were driving home, I asked him what he wanted for lunch. He kept saying what I thought was "home." We went back and forth about a dozen times with this until I realized he was saying "ham" but with a very distinct English accent. You can probably understand why I might confuse the two given that I wasn't expecting him to be saying it with an accent.

My Oldest: He was 4 when we moved and obviously could already speak. I jokingly describe him as bilingual to people. He can speak with an English accent, but he switches it on and off depending on who he's with. I see this happen nearly every day, as he speaks to me one way, then turns to his friends at school and speaks another way. For example, I once heard him say to a friend, "Let me ask my mum." He then came right over to me and said, "Mom, can I play with so and so?" Note the mum and mom. Though I will say, even when he's speaking to me, he definitely has an English manner to his speech, like a slightly different cadence. Another thing we've noticed with him is that when he reads aloud to us, something he learned to do at school over the past few years, his reading voice is much more English-sounding than his regular voice. There are a few other American families that attend the same school and moved around the same time we did, and their children exhibit this same "turn it on/off" behavior.

Another thing I've noticed about the way my children speak is that they use both American and English terms for certain things. They still say French fries, for example, but also know to say chips. They sometimes still say pants to me, but know to say trousers to everyone else. They always say rubbish bin, but they know exactly what I mean when I ask them to collect the trash cans.

Souvenirs from Living in England

I mentioned in my previous post that our time living in England is beginning to end, as my husband transitions to a new job back in the US over the next few months. So as I wrap up this experience, I've been very mindful of what items will remind us of our time living here, which has been nearly 3 years that I consider to be some of the best of our lives.

Antiques

I've bought a few antiques during our stay here and I've also purchased an antique Union Jack flag, which the vendor told me dates back to the 1950s.

Dining Room Table

As we planned to move to England a few years ago, we realized our dining room table would never survive such a voyage. It was a hand-me-down from my parents and had definitely seen better days. So we decided we'd just buy a table when we moved. It took us a while to decide, but we eventually had a table made out of English oak by a local furniture maker. I hope it becomes an item we hand down to our children someday.

Map of Our Village

We spotted an artist at the Burghley Horse Trials (a huge equestrian event local to us) who makes custom silhouettes which are overlaid on vintage maps.

For my husband's birthday this year, I selected a family of four silhouette to be placed over a map of our village. It will remind me of the countless country walks we took as a family in and around our village.

More Wall Hangings

In addition to this piece I ordered, I plan to frame some of my favorite photographs from our time here and create a wall in my new home full of special memories. These will include travel experiences and just day-to-day life. I'm even going to frame the London Tube map we picked up on our very first trip into the city and have used on each trip since! I also want to buy a few prints that a local painter has made of our town to add to my wall.

T-shirt Quilt

I wasn't sure what I wanted my children's souvenirs to be from our many travels around Europe these past few years. We decided to buy them a cheap t-shirt from each country we have visited, and once they've outgrown wearing them, I'm going to have them made into a quilt for each of them.

School Memories

My sons' school celebrated its 40th anniversary this year and commissioned the art teacher to paint a scene from the school. She painted children playing on the back side of the building, a sight I see every single day, both before and after school. I happily purchased that and plan to frame it for my boys. I'm also going to have a pillow made out of my son's school blazer once he has settled back into his school in America as a way of helping him remember his old school.

Christmas Decorations

We never went back to the US for Christmas, so we've spent three Christmas holidays here in the UK. I've purchased several ornaments, including some to give to my kids when they're older. And at my village's Christmas festival last weekend, I purchased Christmas bunting (it spells out C-H-R-I-S-T-M-A-S). Bunting is one of my favorite British styles of décor so it'll be a fun way to incorporate that into my decorating at the holidays.

I still have on my list to buy a full tea set. (I want to be able to serve 4 with cups, saucers, spoons, tea kettle, cake stand, etc.) I've got a day trip in the works to Stoke-on-Trent where much of this is produced and where they have lots of outlets to shop.

I'm not particularly materialistic, and I'm also not a big shopper, but I have been pretty intentional about collecting these things during our time here. I know when we use them, see them on our walls, etc., that we'll always think fondly of our life in England.

What We'll Miss Most About Living in England

Next week, I'll write my final Dispatches from England column for Anglotopia, as my family prepares to move back to the US. Needless to say, I've been reflecting on all that is good about living here (and sometimes reminding myself of the not-so-great, as part of me is also happy to be heading back "home"). I've written before about things we'll miss and what we love (food, phrases, etc.), but here are some big picture things.

The People

From the moment we moved in our house, we knew the commonly heard criticism that English people are cold and unfriendly wasn't always true. Neighbors greeted us and became such a helpful resource to us whenever we had questions about life here. Moms and dads from our boys' school embraced us into their community. My husband's co-workers have become wonderful friends to us. And naturally, it's hard for my young children to contemplate leaving behind their "mates." I've met a wonderful group of fellow American expats living nearby who have been a surrogate family to us when our own families are so far away. We're so grateful for the friendships we have formed and the people we've met along the journey.

The Peacefulness

I'm sure I'd feel differently if I lived in a bustling city or in a high-crime area, but I will really miss the stillness and peacefulness of our life here. I don't intend for this to turn into a debate on gun control, but it is refreshing to wake up most mornings and not hear about murders or shootings. Whenever I've returned from a visit to the US, where I seem to be bombarded with strip malls, giant parking lots, and billboards in my line of vision as I drive, I feel so refreshed by the open countryside around my home.

European Travel at our Backdoor

Oh, the travel, how I will miss it! We've been so lucky to see so much of Europe while we've been here. We were able to drive to quite a lot of regions around Great Britain, and low budget European airlines meant trips to the continent were somewhat affordable, also.

An Intellectual Culture

I don't know quite how to phrase this, and maybe some would disagree with me on this, but here it seems to be popular and well-regarded to be intellectual and smart. Whereas in the US, I often think people are made to feel less "cool" if they pursue intellectual interests (like opera music, or studying history, or reading classical literature). I've sometimes been intimidated by this, realizing I didn't know what people were talking about when finding myself in certain conversations. But overall, I've embraced this, and it has expanded my own interests and leisurely pursuits.

The Scenery and History

You can barely walk a city block or across a field without stumbling upon either amazing history or beautiful vistas (often, both at the same time). Don't get me wrong, I find beauty and history in many places in the US also. But it just seems more exotic here, and certainly older!

Another thing I'll miss? Writing this column. While I sometimes struggled with negative feedback from readers (though now I appreciate my much thicker skin!), not to mention the occasional bout of writer's block, I think knowing that each week I had to share something about life in England with all of you made me more observant and more cognizant of the experience and the changes. As an added plus, I now have a week-by-week diary of sorts from our nearly 3 years here.

My Favorite Memories from Living in England

First, let me clarify that while the Dispatches from England is coming to an end (at least with me as the author), the Anglotopia site is very much here to stay. I hope you'll continue to support the site with your traffic, comments, and sense of community regarding all things Great Britain.

Thanks for all your support and kind words thus far in my journey writing this column. It's bittersweet to be heading back to the US. We miss our families and friends and are happy to be reuniting with them in a few weeks. But we have loved living in England these past 2 ½ years and will miss it greatly. I hope that's been clear in my writing over the weeks (and months and years) in this column.

I wanted to end the column by sharing some of the moments that will live forever in my heart, both because they are special and quintessentially British, and also because they're so symbolic of this journey my family went on.

My youngest son, an avid eater of Heinz baked beans since moving here, was playing a game at our village Christmas festival a few weeks ago. He proudly reported to me, "I just won a tin of beans at tombola!"

The man running the tombola stand quickly added, "There's his tea sorted for tonight!" I couldn't help but laugh, since nearly every word of that would have been unheard of prior to moving here.

Translation for you American readers: He won a can of baked beans at a game similar to a raffle, and the man said that now I've got his dinner for tonight figured out. So funny how our way of communicating varies so greatly between the countries, even though we speak a similar language. We've grown so comfortable with both ways of speaking!

I think that every Saturday I'll get nostalgic for lunch at our village pub. While it's more customary here to go out for a Sunday roast the following day, we always loved walking down to the pub for lunch on Saturdays because it was a bit quieter that day and we didn't need to book ahead. I'll also miss walking down to our village shop when I just needed a few things (or just to treat the kids and let them pick out a "sweetie" and chat with whoever was working there that day).

I think the image I'll most take away from this experience is the sight of my oldest son in his very proper school uniform. Sending him off to school each morning in a cap, blazer, knee socks, etc. seemed so foreign to me at the beginning of this experience, and yet now it feels so comfortable and normal. In fact, I'm more startled when I see what he decides to wear on Saturdays and Sundays because I'm so used to seeing him in his uniform every other day of the week.

Just this morning, I was wandering the nearby town's high street (equivalent to main street in the US), popping in to various shops, holding hands with my sons and picking up the last few items on Christmas lists. I love hearing the fruit and veg seller call out to passersby, I love seeing the market stalls set up on Fridays, and I'll definitely miss the smells wafting from bakeries, coffee shops, and food vans.

I realized how different it will seem to run errands in the US, where I'm often shopping big box stores. In fact, we've grown so accustomed to shopping this way that we have intentionally purchased a home in the US that's within walking distance of our town's center (and cluster of small, independent businesses).

If you've ever moved abroad, especially with young children, you'll know it can be quite stressful. One of my favorite memories from this experience is actually one of my first memories: I walked into our new house and saw it for the first time the day we moved in (and by "move in," I mean walk in with my two sons and four suitcases, which is all the belongings we had for another 6 weeks). We had been living in a hotel for 2 weeks in the US, followed by a week with family, and then a week in a temporary apartment prior to this day (with a 17-month-old and a 4-year-old!) Needless to say, my emotions were pretty shaky by that time. When I saw the view of the fields out my new kitchen window, suddenly all the stress of the past few weeks melted away and I knew everything was going to be fine. And it really was.

Thanks again for following along and reading this column. Answering your questions, hearing about your experiences living in and visiting the UK, and what you love best about British culture have greatly enhanced my own experience. I will periodically be updating my personal blog, Arrows Sent Forth, should you wish to continue following along with our experiences.

Epilogue

One of our last family trips in Europe before we moved back to the US was to the Puglia region of Italy. It is an area still somewhat untouched by tourism. We wanted a really nice lunch for the last day of our trip, so we chose a bistro near the sea in a lovely beach town called Otranto.

During that meal, through a mix of broken English and broken Italian, we managed to understand that our waiter was explaining that we were the first Americans to ever eat at this restaurant. After he walked away, my oldest son said, "But we're only kind of American."

Had I heard him say that in those first few months after we moved to England, it would have shocked me. I would have blared patriotic music in the car and taught him the Pledge of Allegiance, clinging to any shred of American identity that he could grasp at his age. But at that moment, three years later, I realized he was absolutely right, at least from a kid's perspective. He *was* only "kind of" American. And there was nothing wrong with that. I love my country as much as most people. But at some point along the way, I stopped comparing the US to England. If this book had my posts in chronological order instead of by subject that would probably be very clear.

That's one of my biggest takeaways from this experience. No country does something better or worse than another. They just do it differently, and in ways that best fit their culture.

It's what makes our diverse world interesting and fun, and we should embrace these differences.

Am I glad to have the convenience of stores open 24/7, and even on Sunday, now that I'm back in the US? Of course. But I also miss the slower pace of life, the leisurely weekends we experienced in England. It's wonderful to no longer cram my car into itty bitty British parking spaces. But I hate seeing the sea of asphalt in front of each and every store in America.

We make different choices as a family since living abroad. We bought a house within walking distance of my husband's job and my sons' schools here in the US. We are planning to be a one-car family for as long as possible. We eat differently, spend time differently, and think differently because of this experience. I like to say I see the world through "English-tinted" glasses.

I'll always miss England. The people I met fill my memory book with laughs, tears, and smiles we shared together, whether it was over drinks at the pub or cups of tea around kitchen tables. The sight of my son in his proper school uniform, his skinny legs poking out of gray knee socks and shorts, always gave me a moment of joy each morning. I wish I had recorded the sound of people calling my wild child youngest son "cheeky."

But I am happy to be home in the US. We always knew our lives in England were temporary. We missed our families and friends terribly, and we are thoroughly enjoying being near them again.

I love that I finally feel like I can establish roots again, get involved with causes, projects, etc. I think my kids feel that new found sense of permanence in their lives too.

Thanks for reading this compilation of our family's experiences. There were times that my feeling of gratitude for the opportunity to live in England overwhelmed me. How did I get so lucky when so many desire this kind of experience for themselves and never get the chance? I tried to channel that thankfulness into my writing, and to share it with as many people as I could. Please know that we cherished each and every day we had there (even when we were homesick, frustrated and lonely) and that we tried to live them to their fullest.

During a trip to the Lake District in northern England, I saw a poster of Peter Rabbit (a beloved children's book character created by Beatrix Potter, who lived in this region of England). Under Peter's picture, it read very simply, "Be Brave." It was my mantra throughout my experience moving abroad and returning home, and I hope I continue to rely on such wise words. Maybe you will too.